PEOPLE OF VONORE
2020

People of Vonore
2020

COMMISSIONED, PRODUCED & EDITED

BY

THE VONORE HISTORICAL SOCIETY

Published by

People of Vonore
2020

Copyright © 2020 by The Vonore Historical Society
All Rights Reserved

Lead Editor, Matt Deaton, Ph.D.

Book submissions were openly solicited on social media and various outlets through mid-February, 2020. Existing submission update invitations were solicited on Vonore Facebook pages mid-May, 2020.

Special thanks to the individuals and families who took the time to author and update submissions for this 2nd edition.

Published by Notaed Press, Sweetwater, TN

ISBN 978-1-951677-04-6

All proceeds from the sale of *People of Vonore* support the Vonore Heritage Museum. Copies can be purchased at the museum or Amazon.com.

Accepting Submissions for Future Editions

If you would like to include yourself, your family, or someone you love in a future edition of *People of Vonore*, email your typed, digital submission and an optional picture or two to Matt@MattDeaton.com.

Email submissions are preferred, but you can also hand-deliver them to the Vonore Heritage Museum (by the library and City Hall) or mail them to:

The Vonore Historical Society

619 Church St.

Vonore, TN 37885

For all submissions, please mail a $10 per printed page donation to The Vonore Historical Society at the address above. *People of Vonore* is published entirely by volunteers, with all proceeds supporting the Vonore Heritage Museum. If you've never visited, call 423-884-2989 to confirm hours of operation and come see us.

TABLE OF CONTENTS

*Updated 2016 entries indicated with an asterisk (*)
New 2020 entries indicated with two (**)*

From the Editor 9

The People of Vonore

  Barbara "Wolfe" and Charles "Bud" Barnby** 14

  Edna Blankenship 16

  "The Blankenship Boys" by Edna Blankenship ... 18

  Tim Blankenship* 20

  Whitney Deaton Brackett* 22

  The Isaac and Annie Brannon Family** 24

  Jim Carey** 26

  Rusty (Hedrick) Cole* 30

  "How I Found Vonore" by Carole Deaton 32

  Matt and Lisa Deaton* 34

  Jerry Denham* 36

  EmiSunshine 37

  Dave and Janie Evans 39

  Rev. Jack and Maggie Long Franklin** 40

  Luther H. and Mary K. Franklin** 42

  James Paul Graves** 44

Christy and Joe Ben Hall 46
Bill Howe 48
Robert and Jessie Hughes** 50
Fred Isbill 53
Vic and Reba Nell Kirkland* 54
Ritchie and Roberta Lee McConkey Kirkpatrick 56
Reid Lindsey** 59
Dr. Bob and Darlene Lovingood 72
Mike Lowry** 78
Francis and Grace Goddard McCammon** 81
Herman O. McGhee 83
Arthur McKinley Miller 85
Cora Bernice West Miller 88
James "Austin" Miller** 91
Jason and Kristi Miller* 95
Thomas "Beryl" Moser* 98
Kasey Boone Moses 102
"The Family of Cecil and Nancy Proffitt move back to Vonore to Stay" by Nancy Proffitt 104
Dorothy Rex 108
Cory Russell and Family* 110
Lowell Russell* 114

Linda Hitch Shaw 116

Josh and Christian Shedd 117

Mel and Angela Shirk* 118

Tom Steele 120

Larry Summey 122

Paulette Miller Summey 127

Charlie Swift* 130

Clifford and Vicky Jo Breeden Tallent 132

Roger and Lagonda Tipton 135

Brently Roger Tipton 137

Mickie Sue (Barnes) Venable** 140

Frankie Watson 144

Marlene Sloan Willhite** 146

Neil Wolfe** 154

Shelia Wolfe (Janssen)** 156

Violet Wolfe 158

Peggy Delores Morgan Young** 159

A Little History   163

Some Poetry   173

Book Review and Museum Visit Invite   176

FROM THE EDITOR

Today, under the cloud of COVID-19, the people of Vonore long for the good old days. Look no further than Marlene Sloan Willhite's childhood memories of night fishing with her parents, of making (and enjoying) strawberry preserves, or of sneaking through a garden plot to visit her friend Barbara, "thinking that if I didn't go on the road, I wouldn't be in trouble... wrong!"

If you're missing shopping, experience Nancy Proffitt's first trip to Snyder's. "I climbed the old steps to the wooden porch and went into the dry goods part of the store first... surprised to see the tables covered with bolts of cloth which were so pretty... You will not find a small privately owned store like this today."

Or simply enjoy Dillard Craig's fond (and funny) memory of former Vonore Police Chief, Reid Lindsey, baiting him and friends into some late-night juvenile mischief. "We all jumped out of the car and started 'borrowing' watermelons. Just as we started out of the dark field, 'shotgun' blasts were so close to us we all dropped the watermelons and jumped into my 1965 Ford Galaxy. We could still see the flames from the shotgun as we sped away. It was not very long that the 'Feared Reid Lindsey' pulled up just as he did every night. He got out of his car and couldn't contain himself. He laughed so hard that he actually had to sit down on the walkway outside the Gulf Station."

Stories of discovery, adventure and growth. Stories of love, heartbreak and loss. Stories set within national and global events, and a backdrop of covetous natural beauty. Stories common to all humanity, yet shared in our community's unique voice.

This year more than a dozen new entries join the original 2016 submissions including retired Army Colonel, James Paul Graves, former Vonore High School Principal, Mike Lowry, and Vonore Heritage Museum pioneers, Barbara "Wolfe" and Charles "Bud" Barnby.

Sadly, at least two people of Vonore featured in the 2016 edition have passed away – Vic Kirkland and Thomas "Beryl" Moser. They will be dearly missed – already are. Updated original entries are indicated with one asterisk (*). New entries are indicated with two (**).

The world will (eventually) overcome Coronavirus. So will the people of Vonore. They're no doubt making new memories right now, some of which we'll one day print. If you yourself are a person of Vonore, consider sharing your own story. In the meantime, to reminisce, read on.

- *Matt Deaton, Ph.D., Lead Editor, VHS c/o 1995*

May, 2020

THE PEOPLE OF VONORE

Barbara "Wolfe" and Charles "Bud" Barnby**

I am a Vonore High School graduate, class of 1955. When I entered 1st grade in 1943, I along with my brothers and sisters had to walk two miles to school and back. I met my husband, Charles Barnby, in 1957, married and had two sons. We lived in North Canton, Ohio until he retired from General Tire in 1984. We moved to Tennessee in December, 1984.

We both worked with the Vonore Heritage Museum. We really enjoyed this endeavor. The following is in memory of Charles "Bud" Barnby, written by Betty "Griffith" Wolfe, October 20, 2007.

> The world contains gifted people;
> As we are all well aware.
> But when God gave the gift of compassion,
> Bud Barnby seemed to get more than his share.
>
> Bud was a very caring person;
> He could bring a smile when you were low.
> And I know there were times when he as dragging;
> But in his face there was that special glow.
>
> Years were spent driving a school bus
> With Barb close to his side.
> Not all bus drivers have Bud's personality;
> So I know the kids enjoyed their "fun" ride.
>
> Bud decided to take life easy;
> Retire and be his own boss.
> But the Vonore Museum had other plans.
> To waste such outstanding talents would be a terrible loss.

It seems that Bud could do most anything;
Handiwork, organize, and his business expertise was way beyond the label.
And when the ladies at the museum would allow it,
He'd share some fun and laughter with the guys around the table.

October 20th is Bud's birthday;
And the "Grand Opening" of the Vonore Heritage Museum.
While Bud is celebrating with friends and loved ones in Heaven,
We're remembering those special moments spent with him.

Just imagine entering a "Grand Opening,"
And all of life's trials are gone.
And imagine Bud Barnby among the greeters;
To welcome us to our Heavenly home.

EDNA BLANKENSHIP

I started first grade at Citico School. After three months there, my parents, Virgil and Gertie Summey Tallent, bought the property and house where Food City is today. I have one sister, Reba Tallent Kirkland, and two brothers, Richard and Clifford.

We rode our bikes and went swimming behind where the new Food City is now. We have many good memories from there. We rode the school bus to Vonore School and all of us graduated from Vonore High. We had many wonderful teachers who were great role models. Vonore was a very safe and friendly town to grow up in.

When I was a freshman, I went to work for the Teddy Bear across from the high school. I made $3.00 a shift and used

the money for school expenses. I learned good working skills at a very young age, thanks to Lib Kirkland.

I played basketball all four years in high school, and was captain my senior year. Mr. Gordon Sparks, who was VHS principal for several years, was my first coach. Later I had the pleasure of working for Mr. Sparks as a teacher's aide at Vonore Elementary for ten years, then for Foothills Federal Credit Union before retiring.

I have two sons, Tim and Greg Blankenship, both of whom graduated from Vonore High School, as well as Tennessee Tech in Cookeville. Tim is in education (Director of Schools for Monroe County) and Greg is a Mechanical Engineer (with CVG in Vonore).

Vonore was a good place for me to grow up, and for my two sons to raise their families.

With five grandchildren and two step-grandchildren, Edna enjoys reading, crocheting, walking and traveling. She is also the curator of the Vonore Museum, and was a driving force behind the publication of this book. Stop by and see her the next time you're near downtown Vonore.

"THE BLANKENSHIP BOYS"
BY EDNA BLANKENSHIP

When Tim Blankenship was in the 5th grade, Freida Crowe was his teacher. She decided to let the children have a talent show where everyone had to participate, even if they just read a poem, for part of their English grade. Tim sang and picked "Catfish John" and the other children in his class cheered him on.

That afternoon Tim told his younger brother, Greg, he needed to learn to play the mandolin. Greg said he wanted to play the banjo instead, but Tim explained that he had a friend who could already play the banjo, so Greg would have to learn the mandolin so they could have a band for school events and other contests. Greg agreed, and over the years the two have won several awards.

Even today at ages 51 and 48, music is still very important to them, and they play as frequently as they can, often at weddings and funerals. Greg has his own group, "Lakeside," and plays bluegrass gospel most weekends.

TIM BLANKENSHIP*

I consider myself fortunate to have grown up in and to be from Vonore, Tennessee. I attended Vonore schools for my K-12 school career and graduated in 1983 from Vonore High School. Not only did the schools and my teachers prepare me academically, but the community of Vonore also prepared me for life.

As I continued into my collegiate education, my military experience, and my professional career, the lessons I learned in

Vonore have helped me daily. Our community cares about the people there. No matter what you need – a friend, someone to get you back on the right track, a source of help or support, or just a laugh or a friendly smile – you can always count on our community.

The small-town feel that is lacking in many places today was alive and well in Vonore when I was growing up and continues to be so now. Wherever I go, I carry Vonore and the lessons and care I received there in my heart. It is always good to know that wherever I may travel, Vonore is and will always be home.

A retired Tennessee Air National Guard Chief Master Sergeant, Mr. Blankenship served as Director of Monroe County Schools for several years, and then Vonore Middle School's librarian before retiring with over 30 years of service in the Monroe County School System in 2020.

WHITNEY DEATON BRACKETT*

Whitney Deaton Brackett grew up in the Lakeside community near Charlie Hall's store on a horse farm in Doeskin Valley. She attended Vonore Elementary and Junior High, and her freshman year at Vonore High School before transferring to Sequoyah in 1996. At Sequoyah she met and began dating baseball player Brian Brackett.

Whitney cheered for Brian as he played for Sequoyah, then Hiwassee, then Tennessee Tech in Cookeville, where they both attended college.

Whitney and Brian married in 2002, and today they cheer together for their beautiful children who are all three talented and tireless athletes. Their daughters, JuliAnn Marie and Allison Kate, are 17 and 15, and their son, Luke Alan, is 13. JuliAnn plays for the Lady Chiefs basketball team, Allison is a Chiefs cheerleader, and Luke plays catcher for Madisonville Middle's baseball team.

The Bracketts live in Cherokee Circle near the Monroe County Airport, and when not at work (Brian and Whitney both work at JTEKT) they're usually at one of their kids' sports practices, one of their kids' sports games, driving in between, or at church.

THE ISAAC AND ANNIE BRANNON FAMILY**

Isaac Asbury Brannon and wife, Annie Osborne Brannon, lived on Main Street in Vonore and raised their two children there. They had a daughter, Carrie (Wolfe) and a son, Lloyde Parker. Isaac earned his living as a blacksmith.

Lloyde Parker married Letterdee Elizabeth Thompson from Englewood, TN, and they had three children: Lynn Parker, Carrie Helen (Bradish) and Marjorie (Klee), all of whom grew up on Main Street in the Brannon home. They went to

Vonore schools, and all moved away as adults. Carrie and Marjorie both married men from Flint, Michigan, and raised their children there.

Lynn Parker Brannon served 13 years in the United States Air Force. Later, he graduated from East Tennessee State University and opened a travel agency in Johnson City, TN that he operated for 31 years. He is married to Veronica Jeanette Reed from Rockwood, TN.

The Brannon Family remains proud of their Vonore heritage. Several members are buried in the cemetery at the Vonore United Methodist Church.

JIM CAREY**

My name is Jim Carey and I would like to share a few stories of some of the people I knew while growing up in Vonore, Tennessee. Vonore was a very small town and everyone knew everyone in those days. This was a town where you could be spanked for doing mischievous activity by one of the citizens as well as at home. I learned a lot from the citizens of Vonore by observing them and listening to their stories about what they called the good old days.

Jack Samples taught all of us boys how to play baseball, how to read and study the Bible, how to tie different knots with a rope, and many other things that young boys were interested in. He was our Sunday School teacher and he took all of us on a hike one time from Vonore Baptist Church to New Hope Church and Back. That was instrumental in filling up our Sunday School class because we were doing fun stuff. I give Jack and Lena Pratt and my mother (Reva Carey) credit for my accepting Jesus Christ and being Baptized.

I remember our first television which my dad (Hawk Carey) brought home one Saturday. My brother Don and I had never seen a TV before. Well, after hours of putting up an antenna, we finally went in the house to see this 13-inch contraption be turned on. My dad turned the TV on and the first thing we saw was a masked man on a white horse shooting a pistol and saying, "Hi yo, Silver!" My brother and I ran out of the house scared to death.

Floyd (Ned) Kerr hired me to Simoniz his 1953 Buick one time. It took me a week to get started because I took the job not knowing what Simoniz meant. Finally, I was instructed by my uncle Howard Carey that it meant to put a coat of wax on it. I wouldn't ask anyone else because I thought that they thought I was very mechanically inclined when it came to automobiles.

Some of us boys would hang around town in the summertime in the hopes that a famer would come by and ask us to work hauling hay or working in a tobacco patch. If you arrived before 7 a.m. you were sure to get hired at 50 cents per hour. Tommy Strickland and I learned that if we showed up at 8 a.m. after everyone else had gone we could get 75 cents per hour. Our bargaining only lasted about a week, as we became unemployed on most days.

Ben Ray caught my brother Don and me stealing applies from his orchard one day. We were only picking one to eat from the tree and they really tasted good. He fired a double barrel shotgun in the air and shouted for us to come to him. I was scared to death because we had been caught. We went to Ben and he said, "Jimmy go home and tell your momma to come and get all these apples she wants." I went and told her (Reva Carey) and she had me carrying apples as she canned them for days. The apples from Ben's orchard never tasted the same.

I worked for John F. Hall Supply Co. while I was in high school helping Aut Miller and Ronnie Wheeler deliver coal. My job was to assist in unloading the rail cars and putting coal in feed bags so people could buy a sack of coal to get them by until they got the money for coal delivery. One Saturday afternoon while sitting around the pot-bellied stove at Halls Supply Co., Warren Niles said, "Well, I better go home, so Jim, sack me up a sack of coal." As I started the task Warren's brother (John Harry Niles) stopped me. He said, "Warren, why don't you let Jim and Ronnie deliver you a ton of coal so you don't have to buy a sack every day?" You could have heard a pin drop, it got so quiet. Then Warren said, "Well!!! A man might die!" Needless to say, Warren Niles never wanted to die with a ton of coal left in his yard. That was my first lesson on being a conservative.

Reid Lindsey was the constable for the town of Vonore in those days, and I remember one Saturday he got all the boys in Vonore in a group to tell us about a moonshine still located in the Blair Woods. He informed us that the county Sheriff was going to raid and tear down the still the next day and our mission was to rob the still of all the moonshine that night. He said people had heard a panther in the Blair Woods, so if we heard it scream not to be afraid and stay close together as it would not bother us. After we spotted a pile of jugs and grabbed two gallons each, running in the direction of Vonore, we thought war had broke out in the Blair Woods. That was my first experience of so many guns firing at one time. When we all arrived at the Gulf service station in Vonore owned by Rual Kirkland, we were ever so embarrassed to find we had jugs of water. This became a valuable lesson of the danger we could encounter while engaging in illegal activity.

Then the Vietnam War began to escalate, as many of the Vonore boys had to go. The Tellico Dam Project changed the conversation topics around town. The course of history changed right before the citizens of Vonore's eyes. I thank God I was born and raised in Vonore, Tennessee because it made me what I am today. A person who greatly respects the people who have passed away and the ones still living who made Vonore what it was then and what it is today.

RUSTY (HEDRICK) COLE*

Jim Hedrick and I moved here from the San Diego area of California in 1977, and shortly thereafter were married at Vonore Methodist Church by Reverend Walter Barton. I had written letters to chambers of commerce in various areas looking for info on neat places to live, and Maryville's was the first to respond. Jim was retired Navy and we basically picked out a spot on the map near the mountains where we would be able to play our music and enjoy life. We arrived here and bought a house from Bill and Mamie Sue Matoy (the current t-shirt shop on Highway 411) in Vonore rather than Maryville, which turned out to be a very good decision.

Jim and I along with his daughter, Julie Hedrick, came to town that August, and in October we were joined by Jim's sons, Bo and Scott, his daughter, Joy, and my daughter, Grace Marie Lynch. We were blessed by an addition to the family in Melody Dawn Hedrick a year later in October, 1978, so we had his, hers, and ours in our household. The kids all graduated from Vonore High School and went onto their respective choices in life.

When we first moved here Mayor Fizz Tallent welcomed us to town. When he learned of Jim's military background he inquired if he would be interested starting a volunteer fire department. We proceeded to raise funds by having street dances, bake sales, etc. – hence, the Vonore Volunteer

Fire Department was born, and with the help of many volunteers, the fire hall downtown next to the Old City Hall was erected. The original members were Tom Lashley, Pat and Cliff Gerry, Charlie Dotson, Steve Wheeler, Paul Hughes, and Fizz Tallent.

The first fire truck Vonore had was a 1949 American LaFrance. Charlotte Hughes, Jean Tallent and I answered fire calls during the day while the men were working. The American LaFrance fire truck, which I drove, did not have power steering, which turned out to be good work experience.

I've driven a bus for Vonore schools for almost 40 years now (since January 11th, 1982), and have enjoyed traveling all over our beautiful community, taking care of the kids, and watching them grow. I especially enjoy the children of the original kids that I had on my bus and watching them grow also. Vonore turned out to be a fantastic place to raise a family. Jim was even elected to and served on the City Council.

"How I Found Vonore"
by Carole Deaton

"My aunt and uncle have a cabin in the mountains – they've asked us to come & stay a week with them." "That's great!" I squealed. "Where is it?" "I dunno," she replied. "She" was Susie Trotter, a friend, neighbor and schoolmate in the north Knox County community of Powell. It was the 1950s, and we were both 10.

We sat in the back seat of her uncle's Chevy Impala and travelled what seemed like forever down a very straight two-lane highway. Before turning toward the mountains we stopped in a little town named Vonore. It had a 1st through 12th grade school, gas station, motel and a small store. We got supplies there and went on up to the cabin in what I now know as Citico. We had a wonderful time floating down the creek, going to church with the locals and eating her aunt's wonderful cooking. It was a great time.

Little did I know that 20 years later I would be living near that little town. We raised our family there and my children went to that little school.

We were members of Lakeside Baptist Church where Denny Moore was pastor. We bought cokes and bread and ice cream from Charles Hall Grocery (then and still now a landmark).

Both my children, Matt Deaton and Whitney Deaton Brackett, married lifelong Monroe Countians – Lisa Carringer

Deaton and Brian Brackett. They are also raising their families here.

I have great neighbors and friends – one very special friend is Jim Curtis. We are spending the "winter" of our years having a wonderful time together.

When we first came here there was a beautiful wild river running through the valley – now there is a beautiful lake.

Change wasn't easy and I still get angry if I dwell on it. The only thing that is constant is change, my mom once told me. She was right.

MATT AND LISA DEATON*

Matt and Lisa Deaton grew up in the Lakeside community, each about a mile from Charlie Hall's store. After graduating from Vonore High School in 1995, Matt joined the Air Force, and when he transferred to the TN Air Guard in 1998, was taken aback at how his sister Whitney's best friend, Lisa Carringer, who had just graduated from Sequoyah, had grown.

As a result of Lisa's scandalous flirting, they soon fell in love, and in the summer of 2001 she and Matt were married at Oak Grove Baptist Church where Lisa's dad, Steve, is a deacon, and her mother, Barbara, plays piano.

Matt worked several factory jobs before opening Deaton Asphalt Maintenance around 2000, deciding to give college a try in 2001. Ten years later, he'd earned a doctorate in Social & Political Philosophy and Applied Ethics from UT, and had taught at several area colleges including Pellissippi, Carson-Newman, Lee and UT.

Matt and Lisa moved to Knoxville while Matt was finishing his Ph.D. at UT, then to the Baltimore/D.C. area in 2012 for Matt to work as a Presidential Management Fellow at Veterans Affairs Central Office and the Congressional Research Service. They returned to the Vonore area in 2014, renting a log cabin in Corntassel from Bill Howe for a couple of years, then in 2018 moved into their family's "forever home," built on the horse farm where Matt grew up, less than a mile from Lisa's parents, and next door to Matt's mother, Carole.

Their oldest son, Justin, 12, enjoys soccer, reading and fishing. Daughter Emily, 9, loves gymnastics, horses and writing. And youngest son Noah, 5, is into dinosaurs, playing outside and riding bikes.

The Deatons frequent the playground and trail at Vonore Park, enjoy hiking at Fort Loudoun, working out at Monroe County Boxing Club, training at Ogle's Karate, and love going for bike rides at Indian Boundary near Tellico and the Eureka Trail in Athens. Once COVID-19 passes they plan to take a family road trip to the Grand Canyon, and later their first trip overseas, to England and France.

JERRY DENHAM*

Jerry "Mayor D" Denham, who moved to the area in 1999, is blessed with two children, Casey, 21, and Jocy, 15 (pictured below), and two stepsons, Justin, 28, and Shea, 25. A senior engineer at Yamaha Boats, Jerry's true passion is photography. Known for capturing breathtaking angles and effects, his most common subjects are nature and athletes.

Jerry has also been known to referee a Vonore basketball game or two, and is a faithful Vonore and Sequoyah sports fan.

Whether it's a snowcapped mountaintop, a VMS basketball player in mid jump shot, a Sequoyah graduate's senior photos, or a Big Orange touchdown at Neyland, Jerry's work is one of a kind. In fact, his "Sunrise Over Vonore" donned the cover of *People of Vonore 2016*, for which the Vonore Historical Society is very much appreciative.

EmiSunshine

EmiSunshine first began singing in her hometown of Vonore when she was 6 years old. She would sing at a local restaurant on the weekends, churches on Sundays, and has enjoyed many hours with her family at Vonore Park.

Emi began her elementary education at Vonore Elementary School and continues to enjoy the community that she calls home. Supported by so many local fans and neighbors, Emi has an annual Christmas for Families Charity that she founded and supports to help local children with musical instruments and Christmas gifts. With a strong family foundation in Monroe County, Emi is glad to be a part of such a warm and safe community.

She gained national attention at the age of nine when a video of her singing Jimmie Rodgers' "Blue Yodel No. 6" at the Sweetwater Flea Market went viral.

That exposure led to an appearance on the Today Show, followed by touring engagements from coast to coast, as well as half-a-million followers on Facebook. Emi and her family band have performed on the Grand Ole Opry multiple times and have opened concerts for Loretta Lynn, Willie Nelson and Jason Isbell, just to name a few. She's also a veteran of national music festivals like Austin City Limits, MerleFest, Stagecoach and Marty Stuarts' Late Night Jam.

A fourth-generation musician, Emi first sang in public at a friend's wedding at the age of four, and now at age 12, she just released her fourth album, "American Dream," continues to tour the country, and you may have seen her in a national TV commercial for Facebook Live which debuted during the CMAs.

DAVE AND JANIE EVANS

"Coach" Dave Evans, his wife Janie and family are happy to be a part of the Vonore community. Coach taught at Vonore High School from 1978 until it closed in 1995, and ran the basketball program for many years.

His wife Janie is a native of Vonore, and began her teaching career at VHS. Their children Nic and Erin attended Vonore schools.

Coach served as Vonore town alderman from 2009 2014. "All of us have many fond memories of Vonore, and are Blue to the bone."

Rev. Jack and Maggie Long Franklin**

Reverend Jack and Maggie Franklin were born and grew up in North Carolina. [Jack's parents were Henry and Harritt Franklin.]

They migrated to the Toqua Community here in the Vonore area and raised their five children. Bertha, who married Edgar Hicks, Luther, who married Mary Tyler, Evaline, who married Oley McLemore, Arthur, who married Edna McLemore, and Birdie, who married Boyd McLemore. There are a total of about 40 grandchildren.

Jack Franklin Family Row 1- Jack and Maggie
Row 2- Evaline, Bertha and Birdie
Row 3- Arther (Ott) and Luther (Luke)

Jack and Maggie purchased a small farm in the 1920s but could not make the payments when the Great Depression of the 1930s came and lost it. They continued to be tenant farmers for just about all of his working life.

Jack became a Baptist preacher and helped hold revivals all around the area for several years. He was a Master Blacksmith. He made small hand tools, plow points, farm wagons and many handles and other things. He also made caskets.

LUTHER H. AND MARY K. FRANKLIN**

Luther was the second child of Rev. Jack and Maggie Franklin. He married Mary K. Tyler when she was sixteen years old and he was eighteen years old. He was a great father to their seven children, Glesstis Lea, who married Charles Harrill, J. C., who married Joyce McCammon, Robert, who married Billy Millsaps and then Mary Jones, Verlin, who married Ordra Gibby and then Melissa Chambers, Ross, who married Wanda Shirk and then Elisa Lores, Wilma Faye, who married Charles Faircloth and then Fred Tallent, and Roger, who married Heidi Bryan. There are fourteen grandchildren.

LUTHER FRANKLIN FAMILY
J.C., ROSS, WILMA FAYE, ROBERT, ROGER, VERLIN

Luther was a tenant farmer and sawmill worker most of his working life and worked his last several years as a custodian of Vonore Elementary School. He purchased an old house and 3 acres of land at the John M. Carson Farm sale and built a new house on it which the TVA took in the Tellico Dam project. He and Mary then purchased the old Doctor Sharp house in Vonore where they lived their remaining years.

Luther and Mary Franklin

JAMES PAUL GRAVES**

James Paul Graves was born in Vonore in 1937 and attended Vonore schools grades 1-12, graduating from Vonore High School in 1955. After graduation, he was invited to join the football team at ETSC in Johnson City, TN, where he attended from 1955 to 1960, during which time he joined the ROTC. Upon graduation, Graves received a B.S. in Health Education, as well as being commissioned as a 2nd Lieutenant in the U.S. Army. He served in the Army in the 4th Infantry Division at Ft. Lewis, WA, later transferring to the U.S. Army Reserve for the remainder of his 37-year military career. He retired as a Colonel in the U.S. Army.

While at ETSC, James met the love of his life and soulmate, Linda White, from Oak Ridge, TN. They were married in August, 1964 and moved to Rochester, MN, where James Paul was attending the Mayo Clinic School of Physical Therapy, graduating in 1965 and soon after returning to Knoxville, TN, to work as a Therapist at UT Hospital for a year. Graves then accepted an offer to initiate physical therapy services at the Haywood County Hospital, Waynesville, NC, where he stayed until returning to TN in 1971 to also initiate physical therapy services at Blount Memorial Hospital. In 1974, he opened his own private practice, Maryville Physical Therapy, continuing services there until 1997, during which time he also established physical therapy services at Woods Memorial Hospital in Etowah, LeConte Medical Center in Sevierville, and at Family Practice in Madisonville. He retired from practice in 1998.

James Paul and Linda have two grown children, Kristen Colwell in Greenback and Marian Graves Little in Paris, KY, as well as two grandchildren, Katerina and Ivan Colwell. The Graveses continue to reside and enjoy retirement at their home in Maryville.

CHRISTY AND JOE BEN HALL

I moved to Vonore in spring of 1990 and the first time I saw Joe Ben was when I was picking up my brother, Jerome, from football practice. He came up to the car and asked me, "Can I help you?"

First of all, he had a "buzzed" haircut so he's wasn't the most attractive looking person. And second, what teenage boy at a football practice asks a teenage girl, *"Can I help you?"* Needless to say, I was not impressed.

I found out later that day he told the guys on his team, "I'm going to marry that girl someday." And here we are today, 26 years later, married since February, 1993.

We have 3 boys: Joseph 23, Ben 20 and Bradley 18. All followed in their dad's footsteps and played football at Sequoyah High School where they all graduated.

Joseph attended Cleveland State Community College where he has his associate degree in Science and is working his way into the nursing program, currently at Pellissippi State Community College.

Ben thought he would take a stab at college football, and played his freshman year at Carson-Newman College. But he found he didn't like being away from home, and so after finishing his freshman year at Carson-Newman transferred to Pellissippi State.

Bradley just recently graduated from high school and was able to take advantage of the "two years free at a community college" scholarship and is also attending Pellissippi State where he is working on his associate degree. Bradley is undecided at this time on a career choice.

Joe Ben is with Monroe County EMS, where he works hard to save the lives of Monroe Countians, and also drives a dump truck for Hall Brothers Trucking on the side.

We've been happily married for going on 24 years now, and have been blessed with many things, including our boys. Lucky for both of us, Joe Ben turned out to be much more romantic than I initially thought, and his short haircut has grown on me.

BILL HOWE

William E. "Bill" Howe was born in Sweetwater, TN, graduated from Tennessee Military Institute (TMI), spent two years at UT, and served in the Army National Guard. He also worked at Sweetwater Valley Bank for eight years, but since then has been blessed to be in the real estate and auction business, and to have had the pleasure of working with and for the great people of Monroe County.

Bill moved to Vonore, Corntassel Creek, in 1983 and immediately began to enjoy Vonore living. "Being raised water skiing, fishing and hunting, it has been a blessing to enjoy the people, lake and mountains."

"After all these years, I still love to go home, as my wife Terri Jo says, 'beside the still waters of the Tellico Lake.' Thanks for taking me in and loving me – so many great people I can't mention all of you, but you know who you are. *Love God, Love People and Follow Jesus.*"

ROBERT AND JESSIE HUGHES**

The William Robert (W.R.) Hughes Family came to Vonore in 1909. They bought a house on Depot Street. In 1931, they traded this home to Boyd Williams for $200 "boot" and moved to the other side of the railroad tracks. This home was adjacent to the L&N Depot.

William Robert Hughes & wife, Jessie Edmunds Hughes

Robert & Jessie had 10 children. They had 5 boys and 5 girls. They bought the Vonore Telephone Co. from Ben Sloan. The girls ran the switchboard, directing calls, night and day. The boys maintained the poles and lines, installed the phones, and did repairs. Anything that needed to be done… it was 24-7 for the family, for 48 years. The last call was put through the switchboard on Oct 15, 1957. After that, the company was sold to Tellico Telephone Co. and became rotary operated. The family was the communication system for the area of Vonore for many years, and contributed much.

Robert also owned the Jewelry Shop. He repaired and sold jewelry, guns, watches. He was a photographer, developed his own pictures, kept the time and watches for the L&N folks. They came to him for repairs. He invented signaling devices for the crossings, but didn't get a patent. A year later, L&N installed signal devices.

Robert C. Hughes
William Robert & Jessie Hughes
Paul E. Hughes

Robert built a wireless radio. He could talk long distances, possibly England. He knew Morse Code. The FBI & FCC men came to Vonore at the start of WWI. They took parts of the wireless to the bank, made Robert sign, locked them up – inferred that the Hughes were of German descent. This has never been proven. DNA says mostly English. Nevertheless, after the War was over, the wireless parts were returned, with an apology.

The Hughes family has always been proud of Vonore, and proud to be one of its families. Robert passed away in 1958, wife, Jessie, in 1960. The home was then bought by the Russell Brown family in 1962.

Submission written and provided by Susan Hughes Williams

THE HUGHES FAMILY

1957

Morgan, W.R., Stella, Jessie, Pat, Irene, Paul, Annie, Bob, & Alva. Daughter Ida Lee was deceased.

FRED ISBILL

Both of my grandfathers were very involved in shaping early Vonore. They operated businesses in the early 1900s. John Isbill and his brother-in-law owned a general merchandise business, while A.D. Webb was a grocer. Both establishments were burned in the 1920s by a fire which destroyed the town.

I loved growing up in Vonore and spent all of my school years here. Although our school was small, we received a quality education, thanks to the efforts of several qualified and devoted teachers, one of whom was my mother, Sina Mae Isbill. I and both of my siblings, Frank and Lila Mae, are graduates of Vonore High School. My children, Michael and Candace, are also Vonore graduates. Although we all later moved away, Vonore will always be our hometown. My parents, Lyle and Sina Mae, lived their entire lives in Vonore.

I will say, by my standards, Vonore was one of the better places to spend your youth, and there is no doubt that I and my generation grew up in the best of times.

Mr. Isbill was a radio announcer for Vonore sports, graduated from Hiwassee College, served in the Army National Guard from 1959-1966, and retired from Delta Airlines after 36 years. A hunter and fisher, he is proudly married to his wife, Linda.

VIC AND REBA NELL KIRKLAND*

Mr. Kirkland passed away in July of 2019

Vic Kirkland grew up in the Citico community. "I went to school there until my 6th grade year, second semester. Mrs. Sina Mae Isbill was my teacher at VES and she was so good to stay after school and help me catch up on my studies."

As a teenager, Vic worked at the Gulf station, which he would later purchase and operate as the landmark "Vic's Texaco" across from the school for more than four decades. "I made $35 for 7 days of work. After graduating in 1965 I went to Atlanta to work for General Motors. I married my high school sweetheart, Reba Nell Tallent, and we lived in Atlanta for about a year. When we moved back to Vonore I bought the Gulf station."

Reba Nell grew up in Vonore where Food City and Hwy 72 are today. "I worked at the Teddy Bear restaurant through high school, and earned $21 for seven days of work. The Teddy Bear was our 'Happy Days' place."

Reba Nell started dating Vic in her junior year. "I was a cheerleader for VHS for four years and captain my senior year. Every Friday we would get the ladder and go out and decorate the goal posts with crepe paper – really long streamers. Vic was quarterback and captain of the football team. Our senior year we were voted Mr. and Mrs. VHS, and in 1966 we became Mr. and Mrs. Kirkland. We've been married for 50 years."

Vic was owner and operator of Vic's Texaco for 42 of his 50 years married to Reba Nell. Known for a personal touch, the station remained full-service long after most had transitioned to self-service. Reba Nell worked for Vonore Elementary School as secretary for 34 years. Many Vonore Elementary alum remember her warm voice over the school intercom, as well as her friendly smile, regardless of the circumstances behind a student's trip to the office.

Vic and Reba Nell have two daughters, Penny Tipton, who has been a teacher at Madisonville Intermediate for 26 years, and Nikki Kirkland, who has been a banker for 20 years.

Though as a younger man Vic played baseball and was an avid fisher and hunter, in retirement he and Reba Nell spend much of their time reading and watching movies. Among their special accomplishments they note their beloved children, grandchildren, and their faith in God. "We are so proud of our grandchildren Darby, Tori and Hayden."

Ritchie and Roberta Lee McConkey Kirkpatrick

Ritchie M. Kirkpatrick was born in a farmhouse in the Lakeside community near Vonore and attended Lakeside Elementary School. "My parents were Elmo and Grace Wear Kirkpatrick and I have one sister, Violet Wolfe, and one brother, Perry (deceased)."

"I graduated from Vonore High School in 1959 and joined the US Navy shortly afterwards. After graduating from Radar School at Treasure Island in San Francisco, California, I served on the USS Hamner DD 718, a destroyer, where I was later promoted to Second Class Petty Officer."

After the Navy, Ritchie went to Hiwassee College, graduated in 1965, and transferred to the University of Tennessee where he received a BS in Chemical Engineering. "I worked for

Rohm and Haas Chemical Company for 35 years with manufacturing jobs in Fayetteville, North Carolina, Miami, Florida - Latin American Region, Houston, Texas, and Hayward, California, which is near San Francisco, where I was the plant manager. After 10 years, the company moved me back to Houston to oversee the construction of a new plant and be the plant manager."

Ritchie began dating Roberta McConkey while both were attending Hiwassee College, and they were married in 1966.

Roberta Lee McConkey Kirkpatrick was born in Lenoir City, Tennessee, to Henry Robert McConkey and Virginia Lowry McConkey. "I have two sisters, Elizabeth King and Henrietta Pugh (deceased), and one brother Joe McConkey. We lived in Lenoir City where my parents owned a grocery store on the east side. I attended Nichols Elementary School in

Lenoir City through the 6th grade. My dad died when I was in the first grade and Mom sold the store about the time I was finishing the 6th grade."

After her father passed, Roberta's family moved to Vonore to the farm where her mother had grown up. She and her sister, Beth, attended Vonore Schools and graduated from VHS. "I graduated from Vonore High School in 1962 and then attended Hiwassee College through their work/study program, graduating in 1964. After graduation, I worked at Home Federal Savings and Loan and then TVA in Knoxville while attending the University of Tennessee at night. I later graduated from the University of Houston with a BS Degree in Accounting." Roberta eventually retired from FMC Corporation near Houston, where she and Ritchie live today.

Ritchie and Roberta have two daughters, Jeanine and Anita, who were born in North Carolina and both graduated from Texas A&M University. Jeanine is a Chemical Engineer working for Dow Chemical Company and Anita is a CPA working for Ernst & Young, an accounting firm.

REID LINDSEY**

I am Christine Lindsey Goniea. Beulah Brackett Lindsey was my mother, Reid Lindsey was my father, and I want to dedicate this to him. For quite a while he was the Police Chief for the town of Vonore, at times the only law enforcement there, and was such an integral part of our little town for so many years. We moved from the "Soak" Community in about 1959 when I was three, to Depot Street along the railroad tracks (2nd house on the left). I live in Cleveland now but my surviving siblings, Dianne Lindsey McClung and Jim Lindsey still live close by. My brother Reid Clinton, Jr. (deceased), and parents are buried at the Lindsey-Moser Cemetery in the Soak Community, at our old "home place."

In the early 60s my father worked at the Texaco Station in Vonore and later he also drove a school bus off and on whenever there was nobody else to do it. He was elected constable and then appointed Chief of Police of Vonore. I am sure those were the best years of his life because he loved people, loved helping them, and he loved making them laugh.

The following are stories that I have comprised, contributed by Vonore residents and past residents who knew Reid Lindsey well. Some are funny, some are sweet, but all capture a picture of his heart and tell a story of why he was such a beloved man of the Town of Vonore, circa 1958 to 1970s.

COLEEN WHITE CHOATE (cousin): (Note: Coleen's father was Frank White, beloved Monroe County Sheriff for many years and Reid's cousin, and they were very close.) Once when Dad was sheriff we had a lady in booking that pulled out a knife. She was screaming and acting crazy and had the jail staff scared of her and backing away. Reid walked straight towards her, told her he'd been cut and shot before, that she might cut him but it would be the last thing she did! She knew who he was and that he meant it so she shut up and handed him the knife. He looked at the jailer and said, "I think you can handle her from here" and he just walked out! He didn't talk loud or break a sweat; he had control the whole time.

DONNIE SELF: Reid and Dad were good friends from way back. When Dad's brother Gus was in the hospital about to die, we didn't have any phones on Citico, so I guess someone came and told Dad that if he wanted to see his brother he'd better get to the hospital. I can remember going through the underpass at Vonore and all of a sudden here goes Reid by us with lights and siren going and he escorted us to Sweetwater. We didn't stop for red lights or anything. When we got to the parking lot, Reid turned off his lights and siren and went back to Vonore. I never really knew how he knew what was going on, but he did.

After I got out of school and went to work, I think it was 1975 or 1976, my car started leaking gas from the carburetor so I stopped at Ralph Kirkland's garage. Reid was there, pulled out a .38 and removed the bullet. He took the lead out and rolled it down to fit the hole, and it was still in there when I got rid of the car. Smart man and good mechanic.

DILLARD CRAIG: I was in my 2nd year of high school at Vonore and a lot of us would gather after hours, sometimes staying out all night. Someone made the suggestion to go to the Lackey farm and "borrow" a couple of good watermelons. Little did we know, this was a setup deal by Reid Lindsey.

We arrived there around 2:30 a.m. We all jumped out of the car and started "borrowing" watermelons. Just as we started out of the dark field, "shotgun" blasts were so close to us we all dropped the watermelons and jumped into my 1965 Ford Galaxy. We could still see the flames from the shotgun as we sped away. We were shook up and scared that some of us had been hit with the rounds and began checking each other's backsides.

It was not very long that the "Feared Reid Lindsey" pulled up just as he did every night. He got out of his car and couldn't contain himself. He laughed so hard that he actually had to sit down on the walkway outside the Gulf Station. When he finally got able to talk it didn't take long to figure out that he was the "shotgun yielding" rascal!!

After we had time to settle down, Reid went to the trunk of his 1964 Plymouth Fury and pulled out two of the biggest watermelons I had ever seen, went into his cruiser and retrieved salt and a large "butcher knife," still laughing with every cut he made on those melons. After calming down, he gave us a talking to about NOT "borrowing" watermelons. If we ever decided we needed a melon, just give him a call... they were given to him free. I'll never forget that night!

A very true story that has stayed with me for many years...Who would've ever thought that Reid Lindsey is the one person who gave me my interest in Law Enforcement for 46 years of my life! I had the pleasure of working with Reid. I will never forget the cold wintry night he took me to [then] Mayor Blanche Farnsworth's house at 11:45 p.m. and knocked on her door. The sweet lady came to the door in her pajamas and led me and Reid inside where she administered to me the oath of office as a police officer in good ole Vonore! I'll bet not too many could say they were sworn in by a lady mayor in her living room with her pajamas on! She was a great mayor (and a great lady). True story!

KEN LANE: Reid was going to let me drive his race car at Greenback Speedway one night, but I chickened out. I think watching him drive like a wild man scared me to death. But he just said "you are missing some excitement."

[Christine's comment:] Mama said Dad wrecked one night on a dirt track and when the dirt settled the car was upside down and he was standing on top of it. He won many trophies for his racing, which our mama used to prop the windows open on hot nights (ha-ha)... He got no respect at home!

JIM LEMING: He sure was good to us boys. I was out (parking) one night and didn't have any idea anyone was within 10 miles of me when all of a sudden red lights started flashing. Reid let the lights circle a couple of times and then just backed out. He had a good laugh about it the next day. I will never forget that night!

JAMES MCLEMORE: I worked at McCullough's IGA in high school. We opened up one Saturday morning to find that the oil case had been broken into and most of the cans of oil had been stolen, so we called Reid. About two hours later he came back with his car loaded with the cans of oil. He knew who all the thieves in Vonore were!

DEBBY LANE: I remember when he drove our school bus occasionally... boy what a ride! We loved it! I'm pretty sure we went airborne a few times!

ROY SCHRIMSHER: Yes, I too remember the bus rides to school. We got there 20 minutes faster – LOL!!

CINDY LEVINER: My Granny Nichols thought of him as a son because he spent a lot of time there growing up. She and Paw thought the world of him and he them as well. He checked on them regularly both before and after he was police. But he was a mess!! My uncle ran shine off Citico and Reid chased him down the mountain and he even shot at him! When my little old granny found out she gave them both a talking to! (Uncle had his son in the car but Reid didn't know). I also know that he was afraid of the "haint" in Panther Hollow (ha-ha!).

JULIA ROBISON: When Cam and I were dating we would go down in there where the elementary school is today and go parking. Reid knew I had a curfew so he would pull up beside us and sit and talk to us until it was time for me to go home!

EDDIE MAYNARD: In the mid-60s our family would go to the old Clifton Church Christmas programs in Soak. After the program, Santa would come through the door handing out gifts and brown bags of fruit and candy. As a little boy, I was excited to see Santa – the church we attended never had Santa. Of course, my Aunt Phoebe later told me that it was Reid dressed as Santa.

DOLLIE LAMB MILLER: I remember Reid. He drove our school bus. He would fly down those hills and then would look in the rear-view mirror and laugh! We all loved him!

PEGGY HARRISON CURTIS: I remember the bus rides too. I also remember one night after a ballgame he came into the Teddy Bear [restaurant]. He had a piece of paper with a real long number written on it. He said "I think I can remember this number." So I took the paper from him and sure enough he didn't miss one number! I thought to myself, "boy is he smart!" (Which he was!... He repaired Donnie Self's car, didn't he?) But he fessed up. He told me it was his birth date, driver license, social security, and probably his VIN or car tag!

JIM AKINS: I recall seeing him standing up on a motorcycle on 411, riding by the Texaco Station where he worked.

[Christine's comment:] I'm wondering if anyone remembers the time he told us and the townspeople that he would be parachuting out of an airplane into a certain field in Vonore. He gave us the place and the time to be there. The field was lined with cars. We waited, and waited, but finally left disappointed that he hadn't showed up. Of course his tale was, "I did it, but everyone went to the wrong field!"

SANDY SCHAFFER YELLOWEAGLE: My first real memory of Reid was 1st Grade. He was the bus driver and I was running late to catch the bus. I was running to get there. The soles of my sandals had broken just behind the toes and it flopped down, tripping me in the middle of the road in front of the bus.

It scraped up both my knees and they were bleeding. Reid jumped out of the bus and came running to me, scooped me up and carried me onto the bus and sat me down behind him. He got out his handkerchief and I don't know how he wet it or where, but he washed me off and had me hold his hanky on the one knee that was cut up the worst.

When we got to school he told me to sit still until everyone else was off the bus then he carried me into the office and told them what had happened. Next thing I knew, Mrs. Lackey came in and took me to the bathroom and finished cleaning me up. That evening after school when I got back on the bus he told me how proud he was that I didn't cry much when I'd seen that I was bleeding, that I was gonna be a strong and tough woman someday.

I think I walked ten feet off the ground when I got off that bus to go home. I will always be thankful to have known Reid Lindsey.

LARRY JOE LOVINGOOD: One Halloween I was in Vonore helping a few of my friends "decorate" some yards. All was going well until a sorry fellow came by and threw eggs at us and also onto my dad's truck! After I washed the truck real good I set out to find this person who'd thrown those eggs. After a lengthy search I ran across him hiding in some bushes with a case of eggs, waiting for another victim! When he saw me he took off running and I tackled him!

I was in the process of revenge when someone came out of nowhere and got me by the belt, threw me about five yards straight backwards. I rolled across the yard, got up and saw that Reid was the one who'd thrown me, and that startled me because I had no idea that he was even in the world! I thought, "Oh, boy am I in trouble!!"

Reid looked at me and said a few choice words about the "SOB" belongs to him, and for me to go home. Needless to say, I got out of Dodge right then!!! LOL

MITCH SUMMEY: I have a memory of a huge carp wearing lipstick laying on the front seat of the bus right behind Reid. He said if we acted up we would have to sit with the fish!

He also showed up at our door one day with a roadkill cat carcass, yelling at Mom that our dog had killed his favorite cat and that she needed to pay him for the loss of a beloved family member. Absolutely true story! He could only keep a straight face for so long before he broke up laughing. Mom threw a teacup at him!

DONNA DAVIS: I was 13 years old and had no driver's license. I spun gravel leaving the Teddy Bear. Reid ran me down and told me he had to take me to jail. I told him I couldn't go because I had a math test the next day. He laughed and said he was just joking anyway.

ANITA HARRISON HAMBY: Reid was a friend to my dad. When Reid worked as a mechanic at the [Texaco] station he put a transmission in a 1955 Chevrolet for my dad. That is the car that I learned to drive a four-in-the-floor in!!

DIANNE LINDSEY MCCLUNG: A carload of strangers once stopped their car in front of me and Christine as we were walking home from school. Two boys got out and put their arms around us and tried to talk us into going with them. They took off when I told them I'd memorized their tag number and would tell on them. I guess their intention was not to kill us or they'd not have concerned themselves with my memorization skills! I noted their names as they talked to one another and that the one that got out of the car was wearing cowboy boots. We were shook up and told our mom all about it as soon as we got home a very short time later. When dad got home in the middle of the night Mom told him what had happened to us. He didn't wait; he woke up a clerk and had them meet him at the courthouse in Madisonville where they were able to look up the tag number that I had memorized. No computers back then for instant info!

So in the middle of the night Daddy went to the house where two of them lived and got them out of bed, beat them, and took them to jail. Daddy said there was a pair of cowboy boots sitting by the bed like the ones I had described. For the next couple of weeks he went out to the jail and gave the boys a beating and finally the judge let them out of jail.

Dad came to school one day to tell me that the judge wanted to know if that suited me, and that suited me just fine. I was a shy girl, but righteous. I was happy that he'd kicked their butts, and really wouldn't have cared what he did to them so long as I didn't have to talk in front of a bunch of strangers! I wasn't afraid of them trying anything again. Justice served!

Mama said when she married Daddy she thought he was the funniest and most fun man she'd ever known. I'm glad they had those happy years. I've missed his policing "style" a few times when somebody needed straightened out!

BARBARA KIRKLAND: In the 1970s we had our "parking" spot. I was from up Highway 72, and didn't know about Reid, the Vonore Police! But my date was a good old Vonore boy.

He and I were parked under that big oak tree after Vonore Junior Prom and I had all those things on that us ladies wore back then and my dress was long and tight and I couldn't breathe! I wanted out of it as soon as I could. Well, this lady decided this night not to be a lady – I popped the trunk of the 57' Chevrolet Convertible, stood behind it and took off all those tight clothes and put on my shorts and top. It was jet black dark; nobody could see! Relieved, I kissed my date and we just sat there for about an hour and a half. I had an 11 p.m. curfew.

The next evening after school my date and I were eating at the "greasy spoon" and here came Reid. He turned his chair backwards and sat down, put his arms on the table and said, "Well, I see you had a good time last night Barbara. You looked good in that beautiful white dress but it must have gotten a little warm after a while. I don't think your mom and dad would like you changing clothes in the woods, but your date (as he looked at him when leaving, smiling and winking!) was a gentleman." He said "You two are good apples, don't become bad apples, you hear me?"

He knew where all of us kids were at night and wouldn't let us get into trouble! But that next time we went parking, we parked at the old bridge!

BRENDA COOPER MILLER: I remember one time he drove the bus to the skating rink in Niota. *[Note that some Friday or Saturday nights the school provided students transport to the rink on a bus in those days.]* I had never skated and could not even stand up so Reid skated over to me and he held me up and skated a few times around the rink with me. He really could skate good. That was the only time I ever skated. And, sometimes when he drove the school bus he'd stop by the store and let us buy candy or a Coke. Great memories!

CHRISTINE: *A very popular football player back in the day told me that as a teenager he and several friends had been out riding around when they pulled into the Shell Station and Reid pulled up beside them. "I don't know which of you did it but I'm going to be going back over to the school after awhile and I'd better not find that beer can still laying there!" Reid certainly did not find that beer can still laying there!*

My father was a wise man in so many ways. I know a little about his childhood and that it was very difficult at times, and I think that had a lot to do with his ability to empathize with people, but he could also be tough and determined, to put it mildly. He worked to keep Vonore a safe and quiet town. People would say you wouldn't hear a tire screech after 9 o'clock! Vonore was our beloved town for many years. We grew up in an era that can never be duplicated. We young folks had so much freedom to come and go safely, and we had each other and all of the amazing people that were our family as much as they were our neighbors. Us kids were never bored. But we WERE careful. After all, Reid's kids HAD to be! Next year I'll dedicate to my wonderful mother.

DR. BOB AND DARLENE LOVINGOOD

Mayor Bob and Darlene Lovingood have been leaders in education, politics and community organization in Vonore for as long as most locals can remember. Both graduates of Vonore High School have been advocates for children for 30+ years. Together, they have loved and called the children of Monroe County "their own."

Mayor Lovingood's Vonore roots go back to the late 19th century when his great, great grandfather Harmon Lovingood migrated to Monroe County from Hanging Dog, North Carolina. On the town's unique name, "The Cherokee Indians had a settlement near Murphy, North Carolina. My great, great grandparents settled there as well, from Germany. At one point the settlers got into a disagreement with the Indians, and the Indians hung one of the settlers' dogs over the creek." The locals built a church and called it Hanging Dog, hence the town's name. Also in this community was a steel operation that made cannons and bayonets for the Confederacy, which the Union army destroyed during its march through the South. After the Civil War, the Lovingoods' ancestors "came from there to Rural Vale, then settled in various places in Monroe County, including Hopewell."

The Lovingoods have been known in Monroe County for building, making molasses, cabinetry; "believe it or not, even for making brooms," said Darlene. Speaking of Jeff and

Anna Margaret Lovingood, "anything you needed, they made it."

A graduate of VHS in 1968, Mayor Lovingood's first schooling was at Brakebill School, "a two-room schoolhouse" in the Hopewell area. Mayor Lovingood's higher education began at Hiwassee, and he ultimately earned his Ph.D. in Educational Leadership Studies from UT in 1997. His philosophy on leadership is simple: "The key for effective leadership is building positive relationships. The relationship I have with the citizens of Monroe County is based on mutual respect and genuine concern for the students and people of the community."

A longtime educator, Dr. Lovingood taught marketing in both Columbia and Madisonville in the 70s, was principal and Monroe County Vocational School Director from '77-'88, served as Superintendent of Monroe County Schools from '88-'01, then took a post as Superintendent of Christian County Public Schools in Hopkinsville, KY from '01-'08 before returning home. He's even been an adjunct professor, teaching night classes for graduate students at Tennessee Tech University.

Mrs. Lovingood is an accomplished educator as well, retired with over 35 years as a highly skilled educator, including time at Vonore High School. She's been known to teach local kids to swim in the family pool in the afternoon, then inmates how to read at the county jail in the evening. Her patience with students has led to generations of appreciative graduates. "I get notes all the time saying, 'Mrs. Lovingood, I would have never graduated without you.'"

Both Bob and Darlene have many fond memories of their days as educators, and Dr. Lovingood is currently continuing his tenure as a local educator as assistant principal at both Vonore Elementary and Vonore Middle School.

As community organizers the Lovingoods helped form the Hopewell Ruitan Fire Department and the Boys and Girls Club of Monroe County, but they're especially proud of their work with the Military Education Coalition at Fort Campbell, Kentucky. "It was a military initiative for children of deployed service members to support their educational success. The team developed guidelines for schools to provide extra support, counseling and structure for kids while their parents were away defending our country." They worked under the direction of General Richard Cody, Commander of the 101st Airborne Division, on the project, as well as General David Petraeus. On serving with Generals Cody and Petraeus, Mayor Lovingood said, "I learned a great deal from those two men... WOW... could they tell some good stories!" Darlene said of the experience, "We were able to help military children all over the United States."

Bob and Darlene have been blessed with three handsome and talented sons, Robby, Jeffrey, and Andy, as well as a slew of beautiful grandchildren including Zoey, Caroline, Cooper, Catherine, Bailey, Brently, Bella Grace, and Lucas. The lives of dedicated educators and public servants can often put stresses on family life. "Unfortunately sometimes you have to sacrifice time with family to be effective," Bob explained.

Darlene expressed her understanding in this regard. "If you really want to serve, you do everything needed to be better in that capacity. As a dedicated educator, you're giving your time, and your money – it's a real commitment." And she herself has lived that commitment. "We trained ourselves to be better servants. When we needed more training, we went back and got more education, whether a counseling degree, or a special education certification, or a doctorate – whatever it took to help the people we served."

One such sacrifice came in 1988 when Bob was in a heated race for Superintendent of Monroe County Schools. "My opponents, Betty Sparks and Donnie Jenkins, were extremely competitive in the primary, and so too was C.L. Wilson in the general election. I was out campaigning day and night, weekends – almost constantly – and promised Darlene and the boys that win or lose, we would take a vacation to Destin, Florida after the general election in August. I won the election, but was informed that the county school budget showed a $350,000 deficit. The school budget had to be approved by the County Commission and submitted to the state before September 1st. I worked everything out with the County Commissioners before I left by being promised funds from the TVA in lieu of money that would cover the deficit. Just as we saw the 'Welcome to Destin, Florida' sign, the school board secretary, Doris Davis, called telling me the budget was not going to be approved, as had been promised. I turned the car around and headed back home without even putting our feet in the ocean. Upon returning I met with the Commission and the budget problem was resolved, which likely wouldn't have happened had we not returned. We didn't take an out-of-state vacation until I retired in 2001. This is just one example of how demanding a job as CEO of any organization can be!"

Despite the sacrifices, the Lovingoods remain eager to serve the people of Vonore, and thank the citizens of our community for their good will and mutual devotion to our combined success.

MIKE LOWRY**

What could become of a humble Vonore boy who refused to miss a single day in his twelve years of school? For Mike Lowry the future was a large canvas, and education added color to his life.

Born in December of 1953 to John Owen and Lillie Margaret "Tom" Loveday Lowry, Mike was raised to know the value of hard work and a loving family. After graduating from Vonore High School, he attended Hiwassee College and Tennessee Wesleyan before getting his Masters and Educational Specialist in Education Administration at Lincoln Memorial University.

Mike would meet his beloved wife, Jan Henson, between the rows of shelves at the Hiwassee Library as he visited his alma mater to borrow an edition of *Charlotte's Web*. Allan Benton later mused at how radiant Mike was as he described the beautiful Georgia girl he had met. The two youth had both miles and time against them as they pursued their education and early careers. On his visits to Jan's Georgia home, he would sing to her the lyrics of Bob Seger, "*Someday lady you'll accompany me.*" One day, she did. They were married in June of 1981, at a beautiful spring in Chickamauga, Georgia among friends and family. It was a marriage that would last 32 years.

After intense prayers asking God to bless them with a family to love, they had a child in 1989. They named her Mia Sage Lowry and chose to raise her on the family farm. It was on this farm that she would later meet her husband, Bryan Beason. As a child on the land, she was taught hard work to achieve a goal, giving your best is the greatest gift, and that God would always be her very best friend.

As a young teacher, Mike's prayers for family would be answered in another way. He would develop friends that would become like family throughout Monroe County and across Tennessee, the state that he loved so dearly. He fought attitudes and circumstances to guide junior high students to become high schoolers at Vonore High School. He pushed them to launch into the future, to become the responsible citizens he had taught them to be as their Social Studies teacher. Each class had deep meaning and each student held great value.

With the consolidation of Vonore High School and Madisonville High, he was happy to be a part of the committee that wrote the Cherokee Nation requesting permission to name the new high school in the county, Sequoyah. After serving as the last principal of Vonore High School, he created a new family by starting Madisonville Intermediate School. Later, he served as principal in Sweetwater under the direction of Director, Dr. Keith Hickey, where he keenly observed wise leadership. He once again revisited the experiences of youth in junior high and shared in the bright eyes of eagerness as he was a leader of the primary school world.

When not at school, in the field on the farm or with his family, he served as a Wildlife Resources Agency Boating Officer and as a community servant in many other roles including Monroe County Commission. With his involvement in local leadership, he brought those government classes of old to life.

Mike was proud to serve as Monroe County Director of Schools 2007-2013. The great grandson of a Monroe County Director, Mike knew the honor of serving Monroe County's children was not to be taken lightly. He was named 2013 East Tennessee Superintendent of the Year. He truly loved the people that he served and the place in which he was allowed to serve. He called Monroe County, "God's country," stating that, "We live in the perfect location to enjoy God's great beauty."

FRANCIS AND GRACE GODDARD MCCAMMON**

Francis and Grace Goddard McCammon grew up in Blount County and both graduated from Friendsville High School. Francis's father, Oliver Houston ("O.H.") McCammon [Francis's mother was Martha], owned a farm in the Clover Hill Community of Blount County, an area where the McCammons had been present for many years. They sold that farm and bought a farm in the Toqua Community of Monroe County. After the passing of their father, O. H., Francis and his brother Calvin continued to operate the farm.

Francis and Grace raised three girls and a fourth, Lois, passed at the age of 3-1/2 years. Joyce married J. C. Franklin, Marilyn married Clyde Davenport and then Jack Bowers. Carol

FRANCIS McCAMMON FAMILY

Jean married Roy Shults and they had 2 daughters, Barbara Diane and Frances. Barbara married Terry Frank and they had a son, Kory, who is the only great grandchild of Francis and Grace. Barbara D. then married James Brown. Carol Jean then married Glenn Ferguson who had two small sons by a previous marriage.

Francis and Calvin raised beef cattle, sheep and hogs, as well as grains. They did test demonstrations on new types of corn by raising a few rows of several different kinds to see how they produced. They were the first farmers in Tennessee to produce 150 bushels per acre. Francis died the young age of 57 of a heart attack. The TVA took the farm later as part of the Tellico Dam project. Grace moved to Blount County and built a house next door to her daughter Joyce and her husband J. C. Franklin.

Carol Jean, Joyce, Marilyn McCammon

HERMAN O. MCGHEE

Herman McGhee is the son of Bart and Gladys McGhee. He is a graduate of Greenback High School and attended Hiwassee College. In 1963 he joined the U.S. Air Force where he graduated Aircraft Mechanic School and rose to the rank of sergeant.

In his early years, he worked at a psychiatric hospital, then with Greenback Industry, and later went to work on his farm in Vonore on Hwy 72. He said that his sidekick "Wild Man," pictured with him on the left below, is one reason his farming has been so successful.

Herman is committed to public service and has been the bailiff for the Vonore City Court for several years. His hobbies include restoring antique cars, fishing and hunting.

Herman has a large collection of Vonore History with many antique cars, Indian artifacts and much more. In fact, his 1929 Ford Model A appeared in Bell Witch the Movie. He often invites people to visit his private museum, so if you're up his way, stop in and say hello.

ARTHUR MCKINLEY MILLER

Arthur McKinley Miller (Ott) married Cora Bernice West on April 18, 1940. They had 5 children: Charles Kenneth, Wanda Sue Miller Thomas Denham, Paulette Miller Summey, Janet Miller Lynn, and Sheila Miller Summey.

The Millers first lived on an 85-acre farm in the Mt. Zion community bought from Ott's parents, John Oscar Miller and Polly Gentry Miller. One of 12 children, Ott worked for his father, and his dad and brothers sawed the house pattern at a family sawmill used to build his and Cora's home. Three children were born in this house: Kenneth, Wanda and Paulette.

They later moved to a house across from Rose Island in Vonore. Ott worked as a sharecropper for the Henry family who lived in Maryville. They lived there until Paulette was 4 years old. Ott then went to work for John Hall at Hall's Hardware. Before the lake, Hwy 72 ran through downtown, and Hall's Hardware was on the corner of 72 and what's now Hall Street.

The family moved in September, 1952 into a two-story house with a hedgerow around the yard. At 305 Hall Street, the house had been built by the Kidd family in the early 1900s, and is known today simply as "the Kidd house." The house was bought by John Hall and rented to the family for many years. When the Millers moved into the Kidd house the hedges were overgrown, grass was 5 or 6 feet tall, and the home had been neglected for a number of years. Ott and Cora's daughter Paulette says she remembers as a 4-year-old girl running through the grass, which was well over her head, and playing hide and seek with her brother Ken and sister Wanda. She soon became friends with another little girl who visited her grandparents next door, Barbara Cavett Raper.

The home didn't remain neglected for long. Ott was allowed to borrow farm equipment to cut the grass and hedges down to the ground, and Mr. Hall furnished fresh paint. While Cora painted the interior, Ott and other men took care of the exterior.

Paulette's Sister Janet was born in November of that year; then sister Sheila 11 years later. Ott and Cora purchased the house from John Hall in the 1960s and made payments on it until shortly before his death.

Ott worked for John Hall until he passed away on April 29th, 1977. Cora continued to live in the house until illness forced the family to place her in a nursing home in Madisonville. She passed away December 14, 2013. Paulette and Larry bought the house from the family members and later sold it to Chris and Trudie Davis who now own this prestigious house of Vonore history.

CORA BERNICE WEST MILLER

Cora Bernice West Miller was born June 15, 1923 to parents Chester West and Dora Lindsey West. She was one of 10 children. She had brothers William (Bill), John, Charlie, Odis, and sisters Naomi, Eula Mae, Linnie (Lynn), Burlene and a baby girl who died.

Cora 's mother was not a healthy person and died of "leakage of the heart," now known as congestive heart failure, when Cora was 6. Cora found herself as the mom to four younger siblings – 2-month-old Odis, 18-month-old Burlene, 5-year-old Eula Mae, and 4-year-old Lynn – as well as cook for the rest of the family. She would push a wood chair over to the fire burning stove to prepare meals, and remembered their "Grand Pap" (Will West) helping as much as he could.

However, Grand Pap and Cora's dad were loggers by trade and were gone from daylight to dark just to make a dollar to buy food from the Rollin' store that came by their house located up a holler in the "pine flats" between Vonore and Citico.

Cora and the other siblings loved going to church. They would walk to Mt. Zion, Toqua, Citico and other churches if their dad would let them go day or night. They would walk with other families so they always felt safe. She met Arthur Miller at Mt. Zion church and they were married April 18, 1940. They lived with Ott's parents until his father, John Miller, and brothers cut a house pattern from timber on the family's property and built them a 4-room house in the Mt. Zion community.

She gave birth to her son Kenneth and daughters Wanda Sue and Paulette in this house.

The family worked on the farm and for the Carsons. Cora remembers getting up very early every morning and cooking breakfast with Polly Gentry Miller, her mother-in-law, and sisters-in-law Geneva Miller and Minnie Miller, cousins and sisters-in-law Arizona (Zonie) and Renell (Nell) Gray. John and all the boys would eat before they went to work. She said as soon as breakfast was over the women would start cooking lunch and when it was done they would pack it in buckets, boxes, and jars and carry the food and water to the men wherever they were working. It might be at the sawmill, the Carson Farm, Carson Island or the Gentry Farm. Wherever it was, they walked and carried the food to the men. After the men ate the women would eat with the children and carry the containers back home and start cooking supper for when the men came home.

After moving to the Henry Farm across from Rose Island, Cora would help Ott do all the work required to keep the farm going. In 1952 the family moved to a two-story house in Vonore. Their 4th child, Janet Lynn, was born in November of that year. 11 years later their 5th child, Sheila Kaye, was born.

Ott became sick and passed away April 29, 1977. Cora needed to find a way to take care of herself and young daughter, Sheila. She began babysitting and probably took care of most of the children born in Vonore during that time.

Cora was a very strong woman filled with determination and pride in everything she did. She loved all the children she kept and made sure they had plenty of food and naps. They knew Santa lived upstairs at Mrs. Cora's house (the Kidd house) and if they were not good during the year she would tell him.

Cora lived in this house until the family had to place her in a nursing home. She passed away December 14, 2013.

JAMES "AUSTIN" MILLER**

James "Austin" Miller was born July 22, 1946, in Loudon, TN. His parents were Thomas Jones Miller and Minnie Bell White Miller. He had two brothers, Raulston Jones, who was killed in a car accident in 1968, and Boyd, who lives in Vonore. Austin went to Toqua and Vonore Elementary Schools. He graduated from Vonore High School in 1967. He enjoyed playing football, working on the family farm, and working at Vic's Texaco.

Austin was drafted into the U.S. Army shortly after graduation from high school. After completing his basic training he was sent to Vietnam, arriving there on Christmas Day, 1967. He was assigned to Company D, Third Battalion, 12th Infantry of the Fourth Division. He was discharged in June, 1969.

While serving his country he received the Bronze Star Medal with "V" for Valor for heroism in connection with military operations against and armed hostile force in the Republic of Vietnam on May 30, 1968.

Austin married Brenda McSpadden of Madisonville on April 4, 1970. They have two daughters, Krystal Leigh Miller and Whitney Lynn Miller Kerr, and one granddaughter, Madalyn Grace Kerr. Austin and Brenda lived in Madisonville where they raised their family.

While living in Madisonville they attended Notchey Creek Baptist Church where he served as youth leader for a period of time. They moved to his family farm in the Toqua community of Vonore in 2006. He liked to hunt and ride his horse, "Lucky," and you would also see him and his dog, "Babe," riding on his motor scooter. They attended Mount Zion Baptist Church where he spent his childhood after moving to Vonore.

Granddaughter Madalyn was born August 29, 2010. She is the daughter of Whitney Lynn and Matthew Kerr. She was his pride and joy. When she visited, he spent all his time playing with her.

Austin and Brenda spent many days and hours locating and traveling to visit old Army buddies and their families. They also attended many of the Army reunions. In one of their travels they were taken to Batesville, Mississippi, where they met Teresa Jones, the daughter of Clarence Jones, a fellow soldier and close friend, who was killed that day in 1968 on Hill 990. His friendship with Jones and the journey to find his daughter and family was told in the magazine, "Batesville, The Magazine," published in 2013.

Austin worked for Fort Loudon Electric Coop for over 30 years. He enjoyed his work and all the many people he met over the years. He suffered so greatly from PTSD and the memories of the war that he took his own life on May 18, 2016. He was buried with full military honors in Haven Hill Memorial Gardens in Madisonville.

JASON AND KRISTI MILLER*

Jason and Kristi Miller, along with their daughters, Katie and Sarah, are blessed to call Vonore home. They both grew up in Vonore, and from the beginning they knew that Vonore would always be their home.

Jason is the oldest son of Carl and Brenda Miller. His brother Joel and wife JoLynn live in Georgia along with their four children. They are both teachers and Joel coaches football at Cartersville High School. Jason's youngest brother, Jordan, currently lives in Nashville and works at Vanderbilt as a Nurse Anesthetist.

Jason attended Vonore High School where he played basketball, baseball, and football and graduated in 1994. Following high school, Jason attended East Tennessee State University earning a bachelor's of science degree in Chemistry.

Kristi is the only child of Arvid and Sandy Dalton. She grew up in Coker Creek until her family moved to Vonore right before her sixth grade year of school. Kristi attended Vonore High School until the school closed, and she then graduated from Sequoyah High School in 1997. She went to the University of Tennessee, Knoxville where she earned her bachelor's degree in Political Science.

It was while Kristi was at UT that Jason and Kristi's story began. Although they had known each other for many years, and attended the same church growing up, it wasn't until the winter of 1999 that Jason called Kristi to ask her out on a date. From that moment on, they were inseparable. Jason decided to go to pharmacy school in Birmingham, Alabama, and just a year later, Kristi followed after finishing up her degree at UT.

After Kristi's first year in pharmacy school, she and Ja-

son got married and enjoyed their time in Birmingham with friends while finishing school. After graduating pharmacy school, they moved back to Tennessee, ultimately building a home in Vonore, where they now reside.

Jason and Kristi both worked at Little Drugs in Sweetwater with Joe Saffles, though at different times. Under Joe's mentorship, they learned about independent pharmacy. Jason went on to co-own Tellico Drugs, with Joe Saffles and Jeff Anderson. The pharmacy just celebrated their 16-year anniversary.

Similarly, Kristi co-owns, along with Jason and Joe, Vonore Drug, where she is thankful to be able to work so close to home and her children's schools. She and Jason have fond memories of running to "Mike's Market" for a snack while at Vonore High, and now Vonore Drug is located in the same building, between the school and post office on 411.

Jason and Kristi are both very involved in their community. They attend Mount Zion Baptist Church where Jason is a deacon and Sunday School teacher. Jason serves as a school board member for the Monroe County Board of Education and plays the banjo for the gospel bluegrass band, Rocky Flatts. Kristi enjoys gardening, canning, and spending time with her family.

They are incredibly proud of their girls. Their oldest daughter, Katie, is 14 years old and attends Sequoyah High School, where she enjoys playing volleyball and singing in church. Sarah is 11 years old and goes to Vonore Middle. She is very creative and enjoys singing at church and volleyball.

There was never any question where Jason and Kristi wanted to raise their family. They like the saying, "bloom where you are planted," and are so thankful to be "planted" in such a beautiful place in East Tennessee.

Thomas "Beryl" Moser*

Mr. Moser passed away in June of 2017

Thomas "Beryl" Moser was born on his family farm in Vonore in 1933. He graduated from VHS in 1951, and retired as a mail carrier for the city of Maryville after 36 years of service. Mr. Moser is proud to be married to May Moser, and is the proud stepfather of VHS class of 1995 graduate Sherry Summey.

He played football and basketball while a student at Vonore, and later became a familiar voice on Friday nights. "I called football games here for 62 years – quit when I turned 80."

Mr. Moser also served in the Army infantry during the Korean War. Humble about his service, he recalled, "I walked a lot. I got paid for 120 days of combat pay, so they considered that war time, I guess." Mr. Moser said he was honored to have been invited to Washington D.C. to tour the Korean War Memorial and other landmarks as part of the Honor Flight program. "Most of the WWII Veterans had passed, and so they started letting Korean War Vets go. Pretty soon all of them will be gone, too."

When he wasn't delivering mail or calling VHS football games, for more than 40 years Mr. Moser has been the town judge. "At one time, I was one of only five non-attorney judges in the state of Tennessee. You could be a judge without being an attorney, and I'm grandfathered in."

When asked about any memorable cases over which he had presided, Mr. Moser recalled a gentleman in his 70s who proposed an interesting trade in lieu of a fine. "They stopped a fellow one time — an older fellow in an old truck weaving all over the road. They asked him for his driver's license, and he said he didn't have one. They asked if it had expired, and he replied that he'd never had a license, which hadn't been a problem because he had never been stopped. He came to court and said he didn't know if he could pay the fine, but said, 'I have two pigs I can swap you.' I told him, 'I don't have any place to keep two pigs, and even if I did, I don't think I could do that.' I told him I'd dismiss the fine and the court costs if he'd get his license. He said, 'But I can't read or write.' So I told him they're out there every Thursday, and if he'd go out there, I'd take care of it. I called them and they worked with him. About two weeks later he came back and had his license, and he was tickled to death – couldn't have gave him a $100 bill and made him any happier."

Mr. Moser is one many Vonore natives who were forcibly uprooted when the Little Tennessee River became Tellico Lake in the late 70s. He was living in the farmhouse in which he was born, and had no interest in moving. "I was born there on that farm. It's right below Vonore Baptist Church. That tree line at the church – that's where I used to live... It was condemned, and there were fifteen US Marshalls who put me out in the road, and they sold three lots down there for a half a million dollars. Not acres, but *lots*. I was the last one that left."

Mr. Moser explained that TVA bulldozed his family home as soon as he was evicted, and then "put it in a hole." Shortly thereafter, the lake was created, and Vonore forever changed. "They put me out on the 12th of November, and they closed the gates [of the dam] on the 29th of November in '79."

When asked how Vonore has changed, Mr. Moser said, "It's changed a 100%. It's altogether different... Unless you lived here, it's hard to describe. Used to you'd know all of Vonore. Now you don't know a third of them. Like Kahite. Of course, most of them you don't want to know anyway."

Mr. Moser emphasized that while change itself isn't always a bad thing, the way it came about in Vonore is the real issue. "Some people don't like change. I don't like the way it happened here. It was a quiet community, and all this came in – the factories, and all the traffic. It's been a complete turnaround, and I don't like that. When they take your property, and then give [new businesses] a 10-year tax break on it... I got $12,800 for my land, and they sold it for half a million dollars' worth of lots – one lot to someone from Pennsylvania, one from Maryland, and one from Knoxville."

Especially frustrating for Mr. Moser is the fact that far more acreage was taken than necessary. "I'm not for it because they took it and gave it to somebody else. And they took the land the water didn't take... TVA bought 40,000 acres but the lake only covered 14,000 acres... at an average price of $364 per acre. That also included your barn, your houses, whatever – they didn't put anything separate. It was just a flat price for everything... They should have let people keep the land the water didn't cover. It only covered a quarter acre of my land. I'm not the only one – there were 380 families impacted... They should have let us keep what the water didn't cover... People don't understand why I feel towards TVA the way I do. I think that's a good reason."

Mr. Moser is a walking repository of local history. When I mentioned Tom Steele's story about the Strickland boys and the Meigs County football game brawl (see that under Tom Steele's entry), he knew Reese and Reed's names before I could get them out of my mouth, and said he went to school with both of them.

Mr. Moser drives a 1960s era Thunderbird, and when I commented that I was a fan of big body cars like his, he said that once a man told him it would be real nice if he cleaned it up. Mr. Moser asked the man, "Well, do you do that kind of work?" "Oh no," the man replied. "Well then," Mr. Moser said, "you can do two things." "What's that?" asked the man. "Keep your opinion to yourself and your mouth shut."

KASEY BOONE MOSES

"I have a Madisonville address, but I am from Vonore." I have made this statement hundreds, maybe thousands, of times in my life. As a kid I was so embarrassed that I did not have a Vonore zip code. I thought that would mean I was REALLY a part of the Vonore community. I realize now how silly that was.

I look back over the years, and the role the community of Vonore played in my life has been more than a zip code alone could ever offer. My mom and dad, Sam and Sandi Steele Boone, met and fell in love in the halls of Vonore High School. Their subsequent marriage resulted in two Boone girls, Kandice Boone White, and myself *(Kandice is on the left and Kasey the right in their childhood picture below).*

Both Kandice and I attended VES, VJHS, and VHS. Both Mom and Dad instilled in us a great deal of pride in our school, and our roots. We were frequently reminded that we not only represented them, but the community we came from. That has followed me all of my life, and for that I am thankful.

The blessing of being a part of a group of people who not only helped hold me accountable, but have cheered me on with unwavering support as I have made a life here with my husband and sons, has been an invaluable blessing. So yes, I STILL have a Madisonville address, but I am a Vonore girl through and through.

"THE FAMILY OF CECIL AND NANCY PROFFITT MOVE BACK TO VONORE TO STAY" BY NANCY PROFFITT

Wow, has Vonore changed. I first lived in Vonore when I was 12 in an old farmhouse on the dairy farm of KC Roberson with my parents Reford E. Crofts and mother Mary Lena Hawkins Crofts. I remember how much I enjoyed going under the railroad track as my father would blow the horn on our '55 Chevy. Me, my two sisters and two brothers at the time would look forward to Saturday when we would all go to the drive-in theater.

I spent a summer there on the hill overlooking a pretty brick home that had running water. I wanted to live there. Little did I know that I would return in 1972 to live in that brick home. This was the spring before it was to be torn down to make ready for the flood waters of the Tellico project. I was already married to Cecil N. Proffitt, Jr. and 22 years old when we raised hogs on the Starnes farm that was on the river. The farm was flooded as part of the Tellico project but where we raised the hogs can be seen high on the hill overlooking the lake.

I remember the first time I went to Snyder's store in downtown Vonore. I climbed the old steps to the wooden porch and went into the dry goods part of the store first. I was surprised to see the tables covered with bolts of cloth which were so pretty. The other side of the store had a meat counter and shelves of food. You will not find a small privately owned store like this today.

We purchased a home in Vonore in 1978 and Cecil N. Proffitt, Sr. lived there. We moved here in 1981. I raised my family here. Our children, Sam, Sara, and Paul, all went to Vonore Elementary. Sara and Paul also attended VHS and Sequoyah High School.

Cecil Proffitt graduated from Hiwassee College and the UT Department of Agriculture. He worked at the Bank of Madisonville in 1970 when we met. He was one of the five men in the Jaycees of Monroe County that started the Little League for the youths of the county, even before he had children who could participate. He served in the Rockwood National Guard, and started his own business in Vonore, Realty Executives Tri-Star. He was a community leader and sat on the Habitat Board. Cecil passed away on November 12th, 2012. He was a friend to everyone.

Sam Cole Proffitt attended Vonore Elementary School and Mt. Zion Baptist Church. He was born the day after Christmas and once told me he was going back with Santa Clause. I never realized what skills my son had picked up from his parents until one day I was upset with him for something and told him he was going to get punished. He turned to me with both hands out and said, "Now let's talk about this!" He announced at a Little League Football game that he wanted to play, and joined the team for one season. His youth jersey #22 was retired when he was killed in a boating accident in July, 1983.

In the photos below from the top left: Sam, Sara and Paul, Paul in Uniform, Michael and Sara, Cecil Jr. and Cecil Sr., Sam and Paul.

Sara Beth Proffitt married Vonore native Michael Duncan, became a Certified Nursing Assistant, and worked as a cook at local restaurants. She currently works in the deli at Sloan Center in Vonore.

Paul Proffitt completed a course at auctioneer school and passed the real estate exam to be a realtor. He joined the 1st/278th Tennessee National Guard from Lenoir City and served with his unit in Operation Iraqi Freedom (OIF)/Operation Enduring Freedom (OEF) in Iraq in 2004 and 2005. He is a man of faith in Jesus Christ and enjoys the sports of hunting and fishing. Paul is currently working as a journeyman carpenter.

I am Nancy Proffitt and I also graduated from Hiwassee College and UT School of Nursing. I am working as a nurse.

DOROTHY REX

I'm a stalker! At least that's what my son-in-law, Mike, tells everyone.

Hi, my name is Dorothy Rex, and I've lived in Vonore almost a year now. Why am I a stalker? Well, we all lived in Indiana when Mike and my daughter Pat married. Then Mike got a job in Arizona, in the hot desert of Phoenix. Visiting them, I loved the change of scenery, atmosphere, and being by them. So, I moved to Arizona!

Many years later, Mike and Pat decided to move to the high desert in Arizona with my grandson Chris and granddaughter Willow. It's almost 10 degrees cooler there. I liked it there, too, so you guessed it! I moved to the high desert, too (Prescott Valley). Are you starting to get the idea?

Now it's three years later and Mike and Pat are lonesome for trees and greenery. So they moved to Madisonville, Tennessee. I was still enthralled with Arizona and didn't even think about moving, until I realized I was lonesome for family.

So, I now live in Vonore, and you can see why Mike says I'm stalking them!

I have been so blessed by God, my Heavenly Father, to live in America. I've lived in the Midwest, Arizona, Washington state and now in beautiful Vonore, Tennessee.

My first Sunday here, my family took me to Vonore Baptist Church. It was a wonderful experience! I felt at home immediately. The worship was real, meaningful, and the people were so friendly. They found out I like to knit for the Children's Christmas Outreach, and put me to work right away. (I did this in Arizona, too.)

I'm feeling settled here. I love the scenery. Not too fond of the humidity after living in the desert for so long. But I hope Mike and Pat stay here a long, long time!

Ms. Rex has five grandchildren and six great-grandchildren. She is a retired Registered Nurse, and cared for her son, William, a 100% disabled Veteran, who survived on IV fluids for six years before passing.

CORY RUSSELL AND FAMILY*

I was born in Blount County, TN to Larry Rex Russell and Shirley Geneva Shaw. I have one brother, Larry "Lowell" Russell.

Our family was not any different from any other family. My father worked for his brother and cousin at Russell & Abbott Heating and Air, and my mother worked several different jobs as I was growing up until she went to work for Blount Memorial Hospital in housekeeping.

My family and I lived in the small farming community of Law's Chapel in Blount County between Maryville and Walland. My Grandfather, Fred L. Russell, purchased property in the Corntassel Community after the formation of Tellico Lake for his family to vacation on and take weekend trips. We always came to Corntassel for summer vacation and long weekends.

After my grandparents' deaths in 1989, my father inherited the property. We moved that same year and Vonore has been home ever since. I transferred to Vonore Elementary School from Rocky Branch Elementary. After moving to Corntassel, my parents divorced and my mother remarried and moved back to Blount County. My brother and I would stay with our father in Vonore.

As a teenager, I mowed lawns, hauled hay, and cut tobacco in the summers for extra money and sold candy and drinks after lunch for Coach Dave Evans during the schoolyear. I worked for Bob and Priscila Wooldridge at Wooldridge's

Grocery Store for several years through high school, and a few other jobs in between until I graduated from Sequoyah High School in 1997.

I began my career in law enforcement as a police officer for the Town of Vonore in 1999. Eventually, I began working for Sheriff Doug Watson as a Monroe County Sheriff's Deputy and was later hired by the State of TN in January, 2004 where I have had the privilege of being a TN State Trooper ever since.

My wife, Crystal Brown, was born in Dalton, GA, to David & Susan Chapman Brown. Her father was born and raised in Dalton and her mother was born and raised in Tellico Plains. Crystal's family moved to Tellico early in her childhood, and they later relocated to Madisonville where Crystal was raised.

Crystal has one half-brother, David Brown, II, who still resides in Georgia. Crystal's mother, Susan, passed away suddenly at the age of 38 due to lung cancer. Her father was re-married to Sharon Dossett, who had 3 children of her own, John Sands, II, Thomas Sands, and Ashley Sands. Crystal is a 1998 graduate of Sequoyah High School and a 2004 graduate of UTK's College of Social Work. Crystal began working for Peninsula Behavioral Health in college and worked there for many years before beginning work for Chota Community Health Services. From there, she joined the Monroe County Health Council Board and later became a Project Director for the Health Council's Prevention & Wellness Coalition.

I met Crystal in 2002 through her step-sister, Ashley Sands, who was dating a friend of mine. I tried to flirt and be funny to impress her but it went completely wrong. She did not speak to me (nicely) for another 2 years. I asked her out at least 50 times, just to be turned down.

I finally broke lucky and got a date in 2004 and we have been together ever since. Crystal and I married at her dad's and stepmother's home in Madisonville in September, 2005. Our first child, Rex, was born in January, 2008, Kimber was born in July, 2013, and Knox was born in January, 2016.

Crystal and I both enjoy being active in the community and have served on several different boards. After having children, we realized that we needed to be there for them, and so retired from some of our extra activities to spend more time together as a family. We are only blessed with one life. Therefore, we must make the most of the time we have together

2020 update: In 2017 I was promoted to a security detail for Tennessee's Lieutenant Governor. As a result, we have (temporarily) moved to Oak Ridge, but visit Vonore often, and look forward to returning soon.

LOWELL RUSSELL*

Lowell Russell is the son of Larry Russell and Shirley Cooper. He graduated Vonore High School and Roane State Community College with a degree in Criminal Justice. In 1995 he began working at the Monroe County Sheriff's Office until 1998 when he began working for the Tennessee Highway Patrol (THP). He worked there until being injured when his patrol car was hit by a tractor-trailer on, March 13, 2012.

During his career, Lowell graduated from three police academies: Cleveland State Community College's Basic Police Academy, the Tennessee Highway Patrol (THP) Academy, and the Tennessee Bureau of Investigation (TBI) Academy. His THP tenure consisted of 9 years as a trooper and 5 years as a sergeant. Lowell's brother, Cory Russell, is also state trooper.

Lowell's hobbies include flying his airplane, acting (Bell Witch the Movie, The Current and Treasure), running, swimming, politics and writing. He is a member of First Baptist Church in Madisonville, and resides in the Corntassel community.

After the accident in 2012, Lowell wrote *Trial by Fire* which recounts much of his life and lessons learned along the way. He has devoted his life to law enforcement and Veteran programs, and especially to honoring the memory of LCPL Frankie Watson, who was like a brother to him.

2020 update: In 2018 Lowell was honored to be elected to the 111th General Assembly for the Tennessee House of Representatives. He continues to proudly serve the people of portions of Loudon and Monroe Counties, including his beloved hometown of Vonore.

Linda Hitch Shaw

A Vonore High School graduate, Linda Hitch Shaw has been married for 43 years… "to the same husband!" Alan Edward Shaw.

She graduated from East Tennessee State University in 1962, as well as National University in San Diego in 1983 with a master's degree in Business Administration.

Linda was a Naval officer for 22 years, retiring in 1987, and also owned Southwest Search Associates, an engineering recruiting firm from 1991-2002.

Still very active in retirement, Linda plays tennis three times per week, belongs to a bridge club, and volunteers both at a local school to assist slow readers, as well as at a local dog rescue.

JOSH AND CHRISTIAN SHEDD

Josh Shedd was born in 1977 and his family moved to Vonore 1979 where he attended Vonore schools K-12, graduating from VHS in 1995. He bought the old Singleton home which used to be the old Vonore library in 2002 (still owns it today), and in October, 2003 married Christian Lowe Shedd.

Josh and Christian's son, Micah, was born in 2004, they adopted Kimberly Ellington in 2007, and their youngest daughter, Ivy Mae, was born in November of 2015. The Shedds are proud to be living in Vonore today.

"Vonore is definitely a special place for me. I [Josh] have spent my entire life here. I have traveled to several states for work and vacation, and have found nowhere else that compares to our beautiful, loving and super friendly little town. I couldn't imagine raising my family anywhere else."

People of Vonore 2020

MEL AND ANGELA SHIRK*

My Dad is Reid Shirk. He was born in 1939 to parents Herman (Hump) and Lucy Mae Shirk, and is one of nine children. They were born and raised in the Mt. Zion community, in a farmhouse that my Papaw purchased from his uncle.

Tragically, my Papaw was murdered in 1948 when my Dad was only 9 years old. They did the best they could to get by, but ended up having to move to Chicago in the 50s to find steady work. A couple of my uncles stayed up there, but my Dad and the rest couldn't resist the temptation of home any longer, and moved back to Tennessee in the late 60s.

My Dad bought a place in Loudon where he raised my two sisters, my brother, and me. The family farm was still in the Shirk family, split up between Dad and his siblings. Dad was able to purchase everyone's share around 1990. The old farmhouse was remodeled and turned into two apartments about 1994.

Once again, the temptation of home was too much and Dad built a house on the farm in 1996. My youngest sister and I each have a house here now and have families of our own, which makes my and my wife Angela's daughters, Avery Kate and Ember Rose Shirk, the fifth generation Shirk that has been on this farm. You don't really hear of that happening too much anymore, but we're certainly proud of it.

The old farmhouse is now 136 years old and still strong as ever, just as our love for Vonore being our home.

TOM STEELE

During my senior year of 1956, the VHS football game against Meigs County was going badly, and in the third quarter a huge fight broke out. The bleachers on both sides emptied onto the field, and fists were flying everywhere. Coach Gregory tried to stop it. He would break up one fight, turn around and pull the same guy off another man, and then another. After the game coach said, "That's the fightingest man I've ever seen." He didn't know it was two fans, identical twins, Reese and Reed Strickland fighting that day. Meigs won the football game, but we won the fight.

Vonore's last football game that year was with Polk County. They were undefeated and scheduled to play in a bowl game. They were so confident they'd beat us (since Vonore had only won two games) that they wore their practice uniforms to our game, so they'd have their good ones for the bowl game. To their surprise, we beat them 19-6. We were overjoyed and celebrated defeating a good team, as they left crying, learning never to make a Blue Devil mad.

I've always enjoyed athletics and have fond memories of VHS football. In FFA I got involved in boxing and after graduating won the Tennessee Golden Gloves, was on the U.S. Army's boxing team, and later won the Indiana Golden Gloves. I'm now involved in the Senior Olympics, a devoted UT fan, and enjoy a good round of golf. These sports are important to me, but they're all temporary. The most important things in life are my Lord and family. Jesus gave me eternal life, joy, and fulfillment.

I Timothy 4:8: Bodily exercise profiteth little, but godliness is profitable in all things, having promise of life now, and in the life to come.

Mr. Steele and his wife, Leslie, have four children and eight grandchildren. He served in the Army in 1956, '57 and '58, fought with the 7th Core Army Boxing Team in Germany, and also in Indiana, where he worked for Chrysler.

LARRY SUMMEY

Larry L. Summey is the youngest child of Charlie Lee Summey and wife Julia R. Hunt Summey. He had seven siblings RB, Curtis (Curt), Charles, Roscoe, Roberta, Bill and Mary Emma. Larry was born at home in the Citico Community, weighing in at 15 pounds according to midwife Aunt Artie Gentry who delivered him and most of the babies in the Citico area. She said she weighed him twice to make sure.

Larry's father worked for Mr. McSpadden as a sharecropper and later moved the family to Niota. While there Larry attended Niota School. Mr. McSpadden offered Charlie a better house for his family if he would return to Citico and work his farm, so they moved into a larger two-story house in the curve near Citico School. Larry and his older siblings helped their dad with the crops and carried corn to the local mill to grind into cornmeal – the rest was stored in corn cribs for the animals during the winter as food.

Larry and his older sisters and brothers attended the two-room Citico School and played in Citico Creek during summers. This school was closed and he was moved to Vonore Elementary School in the 6th grade.

Larry's mother Judy, or "Granny Judy," as she was known, worked at the Niota Sock Mill for Johnnie Bell Kirkland at the Citico Beach Restaurant where she cooked and loved on everyone who came to the area. She and Johnnie Bell loved working together. If you met them you never forgot either one. Back then, it seemed like the entire area of East Tennessee (or even the USA) spent time on Citico Creek trout fishing, hunting, swimming, picnicking or staying in rental cabins or family owned homes along the creek.

At the age of 15 Larry received a motorcycle for Christmas. His best friend Vic Kirkland had also received one. It seemed every girl in Monroe County, young and old, had a burn spot on the inside of their calf due to contact with the muffler of those motorcycles. He was hit head-on while riding this motorcycle on the Rocky Hollow curves, and spent 6 months in Sweetwater Hospital in traction (that's is what they did for crushed hips in those days).

Larry completed his high school education and received his diploma from Dekalb County, Georgia. While working for General Motors in Atlanta for 12 years he attended Dekalb Junior College and Atlanta Area Tech receiving his Master Electrical License for Commercial and Residential properties. He also owned and operated an auto paint and body repair shop. Larry married Paulette Miller and they moved to Riverdale, Georgia. Their son Sean was born while living there. They moved to McDonough, GA then on to Jonesboro, GA where their daughter Victoria (Tori) was born.

In 1977 the family moved back to Vonore into the house they still live in. Both their children attended and graduated from Vonore Elementary and High School. Larry went into business by purchasing the Texaco service station owned by Ralph Kirkland. He ran it as he had for his older brother Curt while in high school. After a few years, he built a new building, added a deli, and tore down the old station. He changed from Texaco gas to Exxon at that time. Granny Judy ran the deli for him until he sold the station and property to Dave and Trena Etheridge. It is now the Pizzeria Venetia. He built the Wil Sav Drug and later turned it into the strip building for multiple businesses.

Larry worked for Mayor Blanche Farnsworth, Vonore's first female mayor, as Police Chief, and was elected mayor of Vonore himself in 1983. The town received its first grant for Heritage research and the books of Vonore were researched and written during that time. In '84 the town bought the first new police cruiser ever purchased by the city.

Larry was elected to a second term from 1989-91, and during this time negations with Jack Hammontree at TRDA led to a beach being built near the boat ramp. As mayor Larry and County Executive Charles Wilkins worked with Avecor Colorant (now Poly One) owned by Ed Lail and Lynn Klarish to move their corporate headquarters from Los Angeles, CA to Niles Ferry Industrial Park in Vonore. They also secured Dallas Corp (TODCO) led by Bill Mullican, Sr. of Maryville, TN and John Dahl of Dallas Corp, Dallas, TX to build a 7-acre truck trailer flooring plant under roof which produced product in 6 months from breaking ground, also in Niles Ferry Industrial Park. A CDBG grant was secured for the first phase of the sewer system of Vonore. Then with help from Congressman John Duncan, Sr. and Ray McElhaney of Douglas Cherokee, a grant was secured to build the Springbrook Apartments for Elderly and Handicapped. The Springbrook apartments were built while Pearl Lashley was Mayor. Larry also served as Chairman- of the Planning Commission for Pearl Lashley, and as City Judge and Planning Commission Chairman under Mayor Marcus Kennedy.

Elected a third time in 2009-14, Larry acquired the land (40+ acres) known as Heritage Park, boat ramp, beach and ball fields from TVA and Monroe County which extends to the Vonore Middle School, and in 2010 restarted the town's 4th of July Parade. As mayor Larry helped obtain a $250,000 grant for a new ball field, which has just been completed by the present administration. Upon recommendation from Mayor Summey, 3.8 acres were set aside and designated as Veterans Memorial Park by the Board of Aldermen.

Larry worked with County Mayor Tim Yates to locate Food City within the city limits providing 150 new jobs and doubling the sales tax revenue for Vonore. He helped the town receive a $50,000.00 TVA shoreline protection grant for materials and riprap to retain the present shoreline before construction of the flag memorial. Another grant received was for a new fire truck, and he also purchased 3 patrol cars as mayor, which were delivered just before leaving office.

Larry and Paulette have two wonderful grandchildren, Oceana Richards and Hayden Fry. Their son, Sean, is married to Angela Darla Watson, and their daughter, Victoria (Tori), is married to Eric Fry.

PAULETTE MILLER SUMMEY

Paulette Miller Summey was the middle child born to Arthur M. Miller (Ott) and Cora B. West Miller. Charles Kenneth Miller and Wanda Sue Thomas Miller are older, and Janet Miller Lynn and Sheila Kaye Miller Summey are younger.

Paulette was born at home in a house built by her grandfather John O. Miller and Ott's brothers. The house was located in the Mt. Zion community on what's now known as Miller Road. The family moved to a house on the Little Tennessee River across from Rose Island. Ott worked for the Henry family as a sharecropper. Paulette remembers playing along the riverbanks with her older brother and sister and riding a black stallion horse she called "Baldy." She loved this horse so much that if someone needed to find her they usually went to the barn to find her with "Baldy." One day, Ott recalled finding Paulette playing around the feet of the horse when she was about 3 years old. Nearby was a rattlesnake the horse had killed apparently protecting her.

When Paulette was 4 years old the family moved to Vonore. Her dad went to work for John Hall at Hall's Hardware Store. The two-story house they moved into was built by the Kidd family in the early 1900s and had apparently been sitting empty for some years when John Hall bought it. The yard was overgrown and the hedgerow was huge. Ott and Cora, with family members and friends, cut the grass, cleaned the yard, cut the hedges and painted the house inside and out. The house did not have indoor plumbing, and only one water faucet on the back porch.

Paulette made a new friend named Barbara Jean Cavett Raper. They became fast friends and played all over the town. Vonore in the 50s and 60s looked like a Norman Rockwell painting of pride and perfection. Everyone cared about their homes and property and kept everything clean, neat and picturesque. Vonore was a wonderful place to grow up.

After graduating from Vonore High School, Paulette went to work for Levi Strauss in Maryville. After one and a half years she married Larry Summey. They moved to Riverdale, Georgia and she went to work for a mortgage company in downtown Atlanta as a Loan Officer and worked there until their son Sean was born 3 years later. After returning to work the mortgage company moved to the north side of Atlanta so she changed to a new company near their home in McDonough, GA. Later they moved to Jonesboro, GA where their daughter Victoria (Tori) was born.

In 1976 Paulette and Larry decided to move home. They bought property on Greenhill Drive, then a house across from Rose Island built by Hiwassee Land Co., and moved it to the property. After remodeling the house, they moved back to Vonore in 1977 and still live in this house.

Paulette went to work for Sweetwater Valley Bank in the Credit Department and obtained her Real Estate License to sell property, but soon returned as a Mortgage Loan Officer, and later Assistant to County Executive Charles Wilkins. She worked there until the announcement of TODCO building a plant in Vonore. She went to work for Bill Mullican, Sr. as secretary and was promoted to sales as one of the first female sales reps in hardwood flooring in the U.S., and went on to be sales manager for 15 years.

She went to work for a hardwood flooring company in Toronto, Ontario, Canada as International Sales Manager and worked there for 2 years. Tiring of constant travel, Paulette quit this job and then went to work for Rauschert Industries, a custom injection plastic molder as Customer Service Manager then Sales Manager for other custom Injection plastic molders. In 2010 Paulette went to work as Assistant to the Monroe County Mayor Tim Yates until elected as 4th District County Commissioner in 2014.

Paulette and Larry have two wonderful grandchildren, Oceana Lee Richards and William Hayden Fry.

CHARLIE SWIFT*

Charlie Swift attended Vonore Elementary, Junior High, as well as Vonore High School for three years before transferring to Sequoyah where he graduated in 1996.

His father Pete introduced him to the asphalt maintenance industry when he was a teenager, and while he's dabbled in real estate, general contracting, and even served as a Monroe County Sheriff's deputy, Charlie has spent the majority of his professional life growing his business, South-East Asphalt Maintenance. Beginning with a single parking lot line striper, South-East Asphalt is now a full-service sealcoating operation

that does major work for businesses as large as Walmart, as far away as New York.

Charlie is famously ticklish, and has been known to giggle like a schoolgirl when jabbed in his ribs. Being tickled by random strangers is one of Charlie's favorite pastimes, so if you see him out and about (he's the gentleman in the hat), give him a good tickle, and tell him Lowell and Matt sent you.

CLIFFORD AND VICKY JO BREEDEN TALLENT

Clifford Tallent was born on January 24th, 1943 at Tallassee Inn in Monroe County. In fact, he was the last baby to be born at this once popular riverfront resort built two years before the Great Depression that was unable to survive that economic downturn.

Clifford's family – parents Gertie (Summey) and Virgil A. Tallent – lived in Citico until 1950. The picture below is from Citico School. From left to right: Clifford Tallent, Harold Blair, Herman Blair, and Herbert Dupes.

Clifford's family moved from Citco to a spot on Hwy 411 where Food City in Vonore is now located.

Clifford's wife, Vicky Jo Breeden Tallent, was born in Vonore. Her family moved around with her father's job. Frank E. Breeden and Gussie L. (Wilson) Breeden had eight children. Pictured in the photo below are back row left to right: Gussie, Jewel, Vicky, Frankye; front row: Rita, Kathy, Keith, Kenneth (twins) and Gail.

Clifford retired as a belt operator for TVA, has been a deacon at Vaughn Chapel Baptist Church since 1989, and was in the Army from 1968-1970, serving one year in Vietnam.

Clifford and Vicky have two children, Clifford Jason and Kevin Jonathan, and were blessed with grandchildren Victoria Ashley Tallent Gallagher, C.J. Tallent, Jr., and Bethany Ann Tallent, as well as grandchildren-in-law Justin Gallagher and Kiersten C. Patterson Tallent, and great-grandchildren Alexa Hope Tallent and Southern Grace Gallagher.

"We loved growing up in Vonore where everyone knew everyone and all the parents in the neighborhood looked out for all the kids, corrected them if they needed it, and fed them if that's what they needed."

In the picture below, Clifford is with brother Richard standing, his sister Edna, mother Gertie, and sister Reba Nell are seated.

ROGER AND LAGONDA TIPTON

Roger Tipton, wife Lagonda and family are proud to be a part of the Vonore community. Roger graduated from Vonore High School in 1981 and married Lagonda shortly after. They had three children, Amanda Gail, Brently Roger and Patricia Lynn.

Roger served in the United States Army from September, 1981 until January, 1995 and then the United States Army

Reserves from January, 1995 until October, 2003. Roger currently works as a construction superintendent and Lagonda works as a cosmetologist in Vonore.

They have two grandchildren, Alana Gail Millsaps, who cheered for Vonore youth sports for seven years and Sequoyah High School for one year, and Remington Joe Millsaps, who has played football, basketball and baseball for Vonore youth sports for eight years. Passionate Blue Devil fans, they're proud to say, "GO BIG BLUE!!!!"

BRENTLY ROGER TIPTON

4/19/1983 - 7/9/2004

Brently (Brent) Roger Tipton was born to parents Roger and Lagonda Tipton, who are both from Vonore, in Fayetteville, N.C. in 1983 where Roger was serving in the United States Army at Fort Bragg. Brent moved with his parents to Augsburg, Germany, Fort Campbell, Kentucky, and Waterville, Maine.

The Tiptons returned to Vonore in 1994 where Brent attended Vonore Elementary School and then Sequoyah High School where he graduated in 2001.

Brent had two sisters, Amanda Gail (Tipton) Millsaps and Patricia Lynn (Tipton) Harrill. He was the uncle of Alana

Gail Millsaps and Remington Joe Millsaps, and the brother-in-law of Billy Joe Millsaps and Brandon Harrill.

Brently was known by his friends to be daring, fun loving and the life of the party. He was best known by his peers to be a loving, kind and thoughtful young man with a HUGE SMILE that was contagious and an even BIGGER HEART.

The following poem was written by Brently's sister, Amanda Gail, in his honor:

If I knew the last time would be the last,
If I knew your face would all too soon be a memory of the past.
I wish l could tell you I love you one last time & hold you a little longer,
But even with that, I don't know if it would make my heart stronger.
I remember playing all day 'til the sun went down,
Riding bikes, getting dirty, & goofing around.
We could pick on each other, but oddly enough
We had each other's backs when the going got tough.
So many childhood memories we made,
And for that, there is nothing I would trade.
When you get a knock on the door in the middle of the night,
You know deep down inside something isn't right.
Like a bad dream that you can't wake up from,
Your mind goes blank, your body goes numb.
Your knees hit the floor & you're asking God, "Why?"
"Why did you take my brother so soon? Why did he have to die?"

Not a day goes by I don't think of your contagious smile,

How you always gave a helping hand & went that extra mile.

Sometimes a smell, song, or action makes me feel you are around,

And I smile because I know you're in Heaven smiling down.

My little brother, my Guardian Angel watching over me,

Forever in my heart you will always be.

If I knew the last time would be the last,

If I knew your face all too soon would be a memory of the past.

I wish I could tell you I love you & hold you a little longer,

But even with that.... I don't know if it would make my heart stronger.

~Amanda Gail~

MICKIE SUE (BARNES) VENABLE**

Born June 20th of 1935 in Turtle Town, Tennessee, Mickie Sue (Barnes) Venable is the youngest of (Carolyn) Mae Dean and (Lucius) Solon Barnes's seven Children, her six brothers and sisters being Vella (Billie), Owen, Miller, Ward, Quinten and Ruby.

Mickie's family moved to Vonore when she was a toddler, opening and running a saw mill in eastern Monroe County. However, they closed the mill upon winning the bid for running school buses to Vonore Schools.

Mickie attended Vonore Elementary and High School, working summers during early elementary school as a telephone operator. In high school she worked in the office answering phones, helped produce the Blue Devil yearbook, and did plane spotting call-ins. An outstanding student, she graduated Valedictorian of the Vonore High School Class of 1954.

After high school, Mickie attended Cullowhee College, in Western North Carolina. In 1958 she accepted a civil service position in Washington, DC where she met and fell in love with Louis A. B. Venable, Sr., a Private First Class in the USMC. By 1959, she and Louis were married.

During Louis's tours of Vietnam with the Marines in the mid-1960s, Mickie returned home to Vonore, attending East Tennessee State for a teaching degree, and ultimately teaching at Vonore Elementary from the late-60s through 1971. When Louis returned from Vietnam in 1972, the family moved to Camp Lejeune, North Carolina, and then later (mid-70s until 2015) to Parris Island/Beaufort, South Carolina and Charleston, South Carolina where Mickie held various civil service positions until retirement, and also taught computer systems at Beaufort Technical College.

Mickie and GySgt Louis (ret.) raised four children, Dineese Rose Watlington, Aleta Venable Eskridge, Dr. Louis A. B. Venable, Jr. (Senior Pastor, Loris Baptist Church, South Carolina) and Desire' Pearl Venable. They're immensely proud of their seven grandchildren, Dr. Greg Earl Watlington, Jr., Krysta Kara Watlington, Lauren Venable Hammond, Lyndsey Victoria Hobbs, Luke Allen Venable, Victoria Lynn Eskridge,

Charles Dewitt Eskridge, V, and their four great-grandchildren, Solon William Hobbs, Eloise Rose Watlington, Corbin James Hammond and his baby sister, arriving soon.

Mickie served as an assistant Girl Scout Leader at Parris Island, South Carolina, enjoys quilting, sewing, crocheting and reading, was Parris Island's "Drill Instructor Wife of the Year" in 1972, and is a lifetime member of AmVets (spouse). Mickie's brothers all served in WWII, and her brother Ward Barnes served as the mayor of Vonore in the mid-60s.

Sadly, GySgt Louis A. B. Venable passed away in August, 2011 from cancer from Agent Orange sprayed on the jungles of Vietnam. In 2016, Mickie moved to Columbia, SC and currently resides with her daughter, Desire'.

FRANKIE WATSON

04/06/1990 – 09/24/2011

Frankie Watson was the son of Troy Watson and Stacy Couch. He graduated from Sequoyah High School and attended Cleveland State Community College where he studied Criminal Justice. In 2008 he began working at the Monroe County Sheriff's Office until 2009 when he transferred to the Madisonville Police Department (MPD). He worked there until being killed in Afghanistan by a sniper on September 24, 2011 during Operation Enduring Freedom.

Devoted to serving his community and country, Frankie's public service education consisted of graduating Cleveland State Community College's Basic Police Academy (2009) and Marine Corps Parris Island Bootcamp (2010).

Frankie played little league football at Vonore Elementary and lived in Vonore with his close friend and mentor, Lowell Russell, while in high school. His hobbies included football, working out, running, cars, and hanging out at the lake. He was a member of Madisonville Church of God.

After Frankie's passing, the State Legislature named US Hwy 411, through Madisonville City, The LCPL Franklin "Frankie" Watson Memorial Highway. He is dearly missed by friends and family and will never be forgotten.

MARLENE SLOAN WILLHITE**

Memories from growing up in Vonore:

- ❖ Friends were important (especially since I was an only child).
- ❖ Playing with Barbara, Paulette & Janet, Joyce, Freddie, J.W., Jerry, Shirley, Karen, Brenda, Wilma, Donna, Judy, Debbie & Mary Jo, Charlotte & Wanda, Nellie and others who lived close enough to walk to each other's house.
- ❖ Always having at least one dog, from Bulldog to Rat Terrier to American Eskimo to Doberman to lots of "mutts."
- ❖ Granddaddy Sloan holding me on his lap and laughing with me. He died when I was very young and we "sat with his body in his open casket" in the living room of their home until his funeral.
- ❖ Sitting in the swing on Barbara's porch and wishing we had a swing on our porch.
- ❖ Getting a bath in a round galvanized tub (when very young, the bath was outside if the weather was warm enough). In the winter, getting a bath in the same tub in the kitchen since hot water could be heated on the stove and added to the water to keep it warm.
- ❖ Having an outhouse until I was 7. Dad added an inside bathroom that year.
- ❖ Having a cellar where we stored our canned food and potatoes (it was always cool). For years, we would go to the cellar through a trapdoor in the kitchen.
- ❖ Living CLOSE to the railroad tracks but not being bothered by the noise of the many trains coming through Vonore.

- Counting train cars with Mom and Dad while sitting behind our house on the "patio" Dad built.
- As a preschooler, sneaking through the fence and grown-up garden plot to get to Barbara's house (thinking that if I didn't go on the road, I wouldn't be in trouble... wrong)!
- Finding a large "fishing worm" (snake) behind the house, only to see it viciously attacked by my Mom with a hoe when I told her.
- Staying with Granny & Ida or Aunt Thelma before I was old enough to attend school while Mom taught school.
- Being warned over and over not to go into the upstairs "closets" at Granny's since there were only rafters, no floor boards.
- Helping Granny and Aunt Thelma on washday by hanging socks to dry in the fence squares by their houses.
- Helping quilt by standing under the quilt and pushing the needle up where Granny told me.
- Being "flogged" by a big turkey (which I wrongly assumed was a pet) at Aunt Thelma's house and her fury at that turkey.
- Night fishing with Dad and Mom and sleeping under the seat of the boat.
- Being scared by the "mud-puppies" that were hauled into our boat.
- Walking uphill to school with Mom (and making her mad more than once when I stomped in a big water puddle).
- In bad weather, we sometimes were lucky enough to borrow Granny's 49 Plymouth to get to school.
- Riding J.W.'s huge tricycle down the hill at his house and "wrecking" in the gravel.

- Riding a bike to Snyder's General Store to "look & dream."
- Riding a bike to Vonore Drug Store every afternoon to get the newspapers. Mr. Kilpatrick would stack an ice cream cone full of chocolate ripple ice cream for the nickel Mom had given me to spend. Too often I forgot the papers, and Mom would make me go back to get them (so embarrassing!).
- Climbing the trees in our yard and often staying in one of those trees to read a book.
- Anticipating looking in Box 122 in Vonore Post Office to see if we had mail that day and feeling so grown up when I was allowed to learn the combination and open the box.
- Granny Sloan's death while she was staying at my Uncle's and Aunt's house. I remember seeing Daddy close her eyes when we got there and waiting for the funeral home to come get her body.
- Getting my fingers caught in the washer wringers while helping Mom do washing.
- Hanging clothes out to dry using wooden spring clothes pins on long wash lines in our back yard; rushing to get those dry clothes unclipped and in the house when rain threatened!
- Making strawberry preserves late into the night when Daddy would bring home a flat of strawberries (or worse when we had to go pick them!). Then I remember the incredible taste of those preserves all winter.
- Breaking beans to can… so many beans!
- Helping Dad shuck the corn and throw the shucks over the fence to the happy cows waiting in the field behind our house.

- Play house "built" in the tree line behind our house (that space used to be the old railroad tracks but was just trees and weeds at that time). Using only what we found in the woods, we made "table, plates, cups, food."
- Dreading working in the hot garden, but knowing it had to be done.
- Always feeling loved by Dad & Mom (and Aunts & Uncles & Cousins).
- Walking to the pretty brick house behind the old schoolhouse. Loving to go there because the people who lived there would sit on the porch swing and listen to little girls (who probably talked too much).
- Attending Vonore Baptist Church where Cousin Benny introduced me to the LORD one day in Bible School forever changing my life for the better.
- The church being my safe place; there people taught me more about how to love the LORD and the people around me.
- Walking to church unless it was raining.
- Loving the music at church.
- The kind people who encouraged me to play the piano and organ at church even though my skills were not great.
- The day that Mom and I were baptized; Mom had been immersed as a child joining the Methodist Church, but Vonore Baptist would not recognize that baptism so she had to be baptized again.
- The wonderful day that Dad told me God had helped him quit drinking and smoking.

- Dad and Mom's dedication to the Vonore Baptist Church and our LORD after Dad joined the church continues to inspire my life.
- Loving for our youth group to get together with the Methodist Youth on Sunday night because they had a ping-pong table!
- The wonderful years that Mr. Evans was our pastor at Vonore. The Evans family became my second family, and they taught me how to better serve the LORD and other people.
- Dad's stern instructions that I was to treat EVERYONE with respect and that I was no better than anyone else; he taught me with words and deeds to help others if they needed help.
- Helping Mom cook and take food to any family experiencing a death in their family.
- Mom being my best friend as well as my Mom.
- Playing basketball behind the house any time I had time and could get someone to join me.
- Expectations from Dad & Mom that only my best was good enough.
- Strict rules to behave but being allowed to ride my bike around anywhere as long as Dad and Mom knew where I was going and when I would be home.
- Playing in the snow with friends knowing Mom had hot chocolate (and sometimes grilled cheese sandwiches) for all of us when we needed to come in and get warm.
- Mom sewing most of my clothes and pajamas (Once when we went to stay at a cabin while Dad was working in Celina,

I forgot my pajamas and got a "store bought" pair. That was very exciting for this little Vonore girl!).
- Water skiing and staying with Joyce and her family on their houseboat.
- Swimming with friends many summer days at the Madisonville pool.
- Laying out in the sun as a teenager with friends (and my Grandmother telling me that I would regret damaging my skin… she was right!).
- Playing baseball at the old schoolhouse field behind our house. Loving to be with friends, but hating the dust and sweat of the game!
- "Duck and cover" drills in school in case of bombing (since we lived close to Oak Ridge).
- Friends of my parents stopping by and always sitting at the kitchen table to visit (not sure why Vonore friends and family did not sit on our couch or chairs in the living room).
- The agony and horror of watching a friend's house burn.
- The fresh, clean smell of the school building when we started each new year of school.
- Sitting in the hall outside teacher's meetings waiting on Mom.
- Loving to go to school because I could be with friends there.
- The kindness of most teachers, lunch room ladies, and custodians at school.
- Teachers working hard to keep us "in line" and teach their students.
- Praying Psalm 19:14, "Let the words of my mouth, and the meditation of my heart, be acceptable in thy sight, O Lord,

my strength, and my redeemer" each day in Aunt Ruth's fourth grade class.
- Getting a spanking in school (when I admitted to doing something dangerous). When others did not admit their guilt, it felt so unfair. My parents stood up for the teacher!
- A neighbor who had a "rolling store" that he used to deliver groceries and needed supplies to people who lived out in the country.
- Going to the "beauty shop" to get a haircut (and sometimes a permanent for curl)
- Going to Brenda's house, hoping her Mom had made a cake… any cake she made was incredibly good!
- Most neighbors would tell my parents if I misbehaved. "It takes a village to raise a child" certainly applied to growing up in Vonore!
- Waking every day to the wonderful smell of coffee perking (funny that I never learned to enjoy the taste of coffee).
- Naming a new puppy "Charlie" after a favorite teacher, Mr. Charles E. Niles.
- Watching TV during the Cuban Missile Crisis in 1962 praying for resolution, not war.
- On November 22, 1963, crying with classmates after hearing that our President, John F. Kennedy, had been assassinated.
- The horrible day December 16, 1963, that my Mom met me on the way home from basketball practice to tell me that Aunt Ruth and Cousin Randy, had been hit by a train. Losing them brought sadness beyond understanding.
- Watching my family navigate this tragic occurrence taught me how to live life when it seems life is not worth living.

- Believing by our junior year in Vonore High School that W. G. Willhite was the one that I wanted to spend my life with.
- Writing "Mr. & Mrs. W. G. Willhite" in a history notebook that had homework in it. When Mrs. Sheets returned it after grading the work at home, Mr. Sheets had written, "We will see if this is true in 5 years." We kept the notebook and showed him 5 years later (after we had married).
- The worst loneliness of my life when W. G. left for the Air Force in August 1966 after we graduated high school (4 years later, we married at Vonore Baptist Church with Clarence Evans and Billy Joe McCown officiating).
- Being so glad Judy, another Vonore girl, was going to Carson-Newman College in 1966 when I did.
- Grateful to this day (many years later) that God allowed me to grow up in this wonderful place called Vonore.

NEIL WOLFE**

Vonore means a lot to me as there are so many people I know and a lot of them are my relatives. The fall of 1964 I started school at Vonore Elementary in the first grade. I remember the big yellow school bus. Sometimes some snow was on the ground and as my sister, Sheila Gail Wolfe, and I waited under the tool shed, the bus came down the hill at my Grandparent Kirkpatrick's home in Lakeside.

Mr. Maynard Tipton was the bus driver. He was and I am sure still is a wonderful bus driver. He watched out for each of us and he made sure we were seated safely. He was kind and considerate to each of us. It is a pleasure to see and talk to him when I am in Vonore. I rode his bus through third grade. I started fourth grade at Greenback Public School and graduated high school in 1976. My mother, Violet K. Wolfe, started teaching first grade at Greenback in 1967 which at that time she became my "bus driver."

I was born February 2, 1958. My parents brought me home from Blount Memorial Hospital to our home on Rose Island owned by the J.R. Pugh family. I loved that farm helping my dad, Robert Estel Wolfe with all the work. We lived on the Pugh farm until TVA built Tellico Dam and backed up the water over Rose Island and many other acres of good farm land.

Dad and Mom bought a house and six acres of land from Roy and Burma Kennedy on Trigonia Road near our church, Oakland United Methodist.

Farming has always been my love, but I have done other work. I have driven trucks for other employers and had a trucking business of my own. After I went out of the trucking business I have been doing work on local farms—back to what I like doing best.

SHELIA WOLFE (JANSSEN)**

I was born March 15, 1956 to Violet Kirkpatrick Wolfe and Robert E. Wolfe. My first memories were living in the little brown shingle house near Rose Island.

My Dad farmed Rose Island. I remember watching him plow. He would bring arrowheads to us that would just come to the surface of the soil from plowing.

A lot of farm life included the extended families working together. This included hog killing in the colder weather, stirring up lard in the big kettle over the fire, wrapping up pork in freezer paper and salting the big ham to cure in my Grandmother's little house.

Then there was chicken killing and watching the chicken flap around 'til it was gone. Then my Mom and Aunt Imogene would boil the chicken to get the feathers plucked out. Then it would be about ready for supper!

Then there was the tobacco setting out with a hand setter, which was fun (not really). My brother Neil and I would help with that. It was hot when we set it out and cool when we graded it in the barn.

I went to school at Vonore and was in Miss Kidd's first grade class. I loved Miss Kidd and still do. I remember being in Miss Isbill's class, Miss Patterson's class and Miss Betty's class. Miss Betty was one of my favorite teachers, too!

I enjoyed my classmates at Vonore. Some of them were my cousins and that was always fun to be in school with them.

My favorite color of blue will always be the Vonore Blue Devils!

From the Drug store downtown and the Grocery/Hardware store to Thelma's Beauty shop and the Eastern Star/Masonic Lodge, Vonore is a special little town with very special memories.

I'm proud to have had such a nice place to grow up. Even though I graduated from Greenback, I got my start in Vonore. It's part of my heritage!

VIOLET WOLFE

My life has been wonderful from the time I came into this world on February 16, 1933. I had great parents, Elmo and Grace Reid Kirkpatrick and two brothers, Perry and Ritchie Kirkpatrick. We children grew up on a farm and helped with the work. We went to Lakeside Elementary School and then to Vonore High School.

It was at Vonore High School that I met my future husband, Robert Estel Wolfe. He graduated in 1950 and I graduated in 1951. He worked with his dad on the Jim Pugh farm. After I graduated, we got married on May 25, 1951.

On March 15, 1956 a baby girl was born to us, Sheila Gail Wolfe. Then two years later our son Robert Neil Wolfe was born. We lived on the Pugh farm until 1968. The Tellico Dam was in the process of being built, so we had to move. We bought property in the Trigonia community. Estel was working for Dixie Roller Mills in Madisonville and I enrolled in classes at Hiwassee College. The children were attending Vonore Elementary School.

After I graduated from Hiwassee College I attended the University of Tennessee for two years, receiving a degree in Elementary Education. I taught first grade for twenty-eight years at Greenback Public School.

PEGGY DELORES MORGAN YOUNG**

My name is Peggy Delores Morgan, and I was born on October 21, 1934 in the Lakeside community. My mother is Roxie Hodge, and my father is Theodore R. Morgan. My grandmother was Callie Lee McNabb, and my grandfather was Joe C. Hodge. My father left for North Carolina to look for a job and never returned. I was fifteen months old. My sister Margaret was six years old. After that we lived with our grandparents. We called them Granny and Pap. We had a thirty-acre farm. We grew corn, tobacco, and always a large garden. All the vegetables you can name. I would hoe the okra, corn, beans, and tomatoes and do many chores after I grew.

I always loved music. My mother said I would sing before I could talk, but she knew the melody I was singing.

After I was old enough, I walked to Vonore to Sarah Jones's for piano lessons every Saturday. When I was four years old I went to a three room school at Lakeside. I was too young to register, but I was allowed to stay in the primary, first and second grades where Nary Lena Sheets would have me go to the music room, and she would teach me songs at recess.

When I was in the fifth grade we sold the farm and moved to Vonore in the old Dr. Hannah's house.

But then my mother and father were divorced, and mother married James O. Cavett. They had two daughters – Jo Annett and Barbara Jean.

We all lived together, and my grandmother was a wonderful cook. I would never invite my boyfriends to eat as I thought they had much better than me. As years passed I knew I had the best.

In high school I took piano lessons from Mrs. Rena Jones and sang at many functions. Then I went to Maryville College and took voice lessons from Dr. Harry Harthart. I sang at many weddings.

I always loved school. Mrs. Ruth Raye was a wonderful teacher, and Mr. Jonny Kennedy was too. Mrs. Jones was great in music, and Jason, her husband, was basketball coach, and also John Q. Wilburn. They called him "Nig" as he had dark skin (so handsome). I played on the basketball team, and when I was a senior I was awarded Best Girl Athlete. I also played the trombone in the band.

After high school I went to East Tennessee State College. I auditioned for the college band and was accepted. I got a job at the cafeteria serving the football team at 35 cents an hour. Later I changed jobs and worked for the school nurse and doctors. I sang in the Glee Club (choir). As time went on I learned to play many instruments.

My teacher, Mr. Lindley, said I had done well with the violin, and wanted me to join the orchestra. So I was in the marching band, the concert band, and the orchestra.

I auditioned for a Broadway show on campus, and after singing three notes I was accepted. It was a big hit.

I was on summer break from college when I met Hollis Young. Eight of us girls were at Barbara Jenkins's house for a slumber party. Hollis came to bring Jane Kennedy's sweater to her, as she had left it in his car. The next day he sent his friend to my home to ask me for a date and I went out with Hollis. We married a year later.

We have three children – David, Jeffrey, and Nancy Cara. David has two children – John and Holly. John works for the government at Warner Air Force Base (a genius). Getting his Master's degree, his papers are so good they put them in the library for reference. Jeffrey has four children – Wil, Jake, Matthew and Lee. Nancy has three children – Greg, Bobby and Brent (twins). The twins graduate from college soon. Bobby has an internship at a CPA firm in Atlanta and Brent will do church work. Wil Young works for the Sheriff's Department. Jake's in landscaping. Matthew works on the dairy farm. Lee is still in high school.

I have had many jobs since I married. I taught school at Vonore, directed the band, and public school music. After moving to Cleveland there were no music teachers in the schools, so I got out of music. So I've been a bank bookkeeper – payroll person, account executive for a television station. I worked marketing at Photography for Coppingers. That was my calling. I traveled to Dallas, TX, St. Louis, MO, Memphis, TN, Nashville, TN, Atlanta, GA, and booked photographic dates, and taught in Portland, OR.

I worked for Meyers Photography, and I enjoyed that. He paid me what I was worth. I made more in a week than I made in a year teaching.

After I retired in 1999, my husband had cancer. That was a nightmare, and he died in 2009. In the meanwhile I had lung cancer. But Dr. Daniel Karp at the MD Anderson Cancer Center in Houston, TX saved my life. I am cured of lung cancer.

I am grateful for what I have and the places I've been: Alaska twice, California three times, Arizona, Reno, Nevada, Cape Cod, Massachusetts. I've had a good life in spite of my daddy. I was grateful for my Grandma and Papa – we were buddies. I always wanted to be rich, but I find I'm the richest of all with my wonderful family.

I'm now eighty-two and life disappears in front of your eyes. I was sixteen yesterday.

A LITTLE HISTORY

The below picture is from a newspaper clipping on the Tallassee Inn, a weekend resort once in Citico, submitted by Clifford Tallent. Mr. Tallent's parents rented the Inn after it closed, and he was born there in 1943.

A porch at Tallassee Inn offered guests a good view of the countryside and Little Tennessee River.

The below picture is of Vonore Elementary, Jr. High and High Schools, taken in roughly 1992. The press box from which Beryl Moser called games can be seen to the right of the buses arranged for afternoon departure (one of which Rusty (Hedrick) Cole was likely driving), Vic Kirkland's Texaco station can be seen on the left of the two-lane 411, the "new gym" where Dave Evans coached hundreds of Blue Devil basketball games can be seen at bottom left, and "Mike's Market," which is now Jason and Kristi Miller's Vonore Drug, can be seen between the post office and school – thanks to Tabby Arden for sharing this photo.

People of Vonore 2020

The following brief account of early Vonore history was shared by Brenda Tipton, apparently written by the now deceased A. J. Kennedy some time ago. For more in-depth study of Vonore history, several books, including Vonore: Yesterday and Today, can be reviewed or purchased at the Vonore Museum at 611 Church Street.

After the Treaty of 1819 with the Cherokee Indians, new lands were opened for sale between the Hiwassee and Little Tennessee Rivers. This brought an influx of white settlers. One of the stipulations in the treaty was that no one person could purchase more than 640 acres, nor could one of his children own more than 320 acres, and no land was to be sold for less than $2 per acre. Most of the settlers came from Blount County and North Carolina. Some white settlers had already purchased land from the Indians and were living in the Indian Territory. These people were permitted to retain their property.

Some of the pioneer families that settled in the immediate vicinity of Vonore included: Blair, Upton, Hall, Kinser, Humes, Brakebill, Birchfield, Swaney, Tipton, Harvey, Grayson, Isbill, Moser, Dawson, Lattimore, McKeehan, Starritt, Lowry, Sloan, Snider, Wear, Holloway, Marshall, Leslie, Jenkins, Garren, Summitt, Johnston, Milligan, Millsaps, Hitch, Niles, Kennedy, Lowe, Underwood, Hughes, Brannon, Carver, Ray, Clemmer, Pettit, Sheets, Samples, Huff, Kerr, Harrison, Bingham, Berrong, Webb, Gerding, Woody,

McGhee, Pace, Keyees, Hammontree, Watson, Howard, Kirkpatrick, Cansler, Davis, Thompson, Peeler, Gray, Shadden, McMillian, Wiggins, Farr, Arp, Hill, Rollins, Robinson, Curtiss, Myers, Carson, Moree, McCollum, Wayman, Pressley, Chambers, Hutchinson, Henry, Rodgers, Henley, Carey, Regan, Brookshire, Fultz, Axley, Sharp, Dotson, Farnsworth, Anderson, Rasar, Tallent, Kirkland, White, Cunningham, Plyley, Williams, Mullins, Cline, and Blankenship. There may be many other families recorded which cannot be recalled.

At the time of the Hiwassee Purchase there were no roads, only Indian trails, and the predominant mode of travel was by pack horse. Wagon roads were not established until years later. With all the new settlers coming in there was demand for goods of all kinds. These goods were shipped by the water route. The community of Morganton had been established on the north side of the Little Tennessee River, which was about as far as civilization had advanced. From here the settlers received their supplies after the War Between the States. The farming industry grew rapidly and the coming of the railroads changed the supply routes.

The Atlanta, Knoxville, and Northern Railroad was built in 1890. This was the beginning of the Town of Vonore, and as it was located in a prosperous farming area, a depot and sidetrack were built.

The station was known as "Upton," named for the Upton family who had owned the surrounding land. The Uptons sold their property to the county and the county poorhouse was established in 1882.

The county sold the property to C. F. Lattimore and J. C. Hall on September 26, 1891, and in 1892 Lattimore sold his interest to J. C. Hall. The town was laid out parallel with the railroad by Hall and Kennedy. There was some difficulty delivering freight due to confusion from the name Upton, as there was an Uptonville, Tennessee. Furthermore, there was a young medical doctor who had come to practice medicine, and there was a delay in receiving medicine from Knoxville as the community received its mail from Madisonville. So there was a great need for a post office, and Dr. W. B. Kennedy set out to get this done.

In naming the town, the community wished to honor General Crawford Vaughn, who was an outstanding general in the Confederate Army from Monroe County, but there was already a Vaughn, Tennessee. Dr. Kennedy suggested the name Vonore with "von" being a German preposition meaning "of," and "ore" referring to fabulous tales told by prospectors in search of ore in the nearby mountains. The Vonore Post Office was established on September 30, 1893, with Walter B. Kennedy appointed as first postmaster.

The town began to grow rapidly in 1892, and a store was built by Hall and Kennedy which was burned by a dissatisfied customer. Frank Kinser built the next store near the site of the Atlanta, Knoxville, and Northern Railroad Station. Lee R.

Sloan built the next one and handled hardware supplies. Hamp Millsaps built the next one handling dry goods.

In the early 1900s, the Atlanta, Knoxville, and Northern Railroad was having financial trouble placing a bridge across the Tennessee River in Knoxville. The Louisville and Nashville Railroad purchased the company in 1902 and began to improve the road bed. A new route survey was made through Vonore, which changed the location of the tracks.

When this happened the streets were crisscrossed and ruined the plan of the town, changing the roads and streets from which the town never recovered. A new depot was built east of the town, and as activity began to move to the new station, the old buildings fell into poor repair, and brought in low rent dwellers, which is still a shadow of the past. Five new stores were built rapidly increasing the growth and economic life of the town. Many new houses were built and the population doubled in a short time. Transportation by water had lost to the railroads by this time and you could no longer see the steamboats plowing the mighty Little Tennessee River.

With the coming of the automobile, this too changed the town. There were great demands for better roads. A new state highway was built above the town in 1933, and this caused fast migration, as the railroad no longer gave service for passengers or freight. Soon the depot was torn down and moved. As a result of no mail service, all supplies and mail were brought in by truck. The new highway caused a mad scramble, and the town's landscape changed yet again.

Now [written in the 70s] the Tennessee Valley Authority has ascended on our borders and we are in the process of moving again. They have new plans for reconstruction and the building of a new Vonore. TVA is assisting in several programs, such as helping merchants finance new stores, building a waterfront, boat docks, planning of new industries, city hall, and a water system. They estimate the growth of population will be from 25 to 40 thousand in the next 25 years.

Through the efforts of A. J. Kennedy, the town of Vonore was incorporated in 1965. Ward Barnes was elected mayor, and Jack Samples and Earl James Hutton were elected aldermen. Under this regime streetlights were installed and roads improved, which made our little town look more like a city. In 1967, Ward Barnes was elected mayor, and Mrs. Blanche Farnsworth and Tom Moser were elected aldermen. In 1969, Mrs. Blanche Farnsworth was elected mayor, and Jack Hawk and James Brown were elected aldermen. In 1971, Mrs. Farnsworth was re-elected mayor, and James Brown and Harry Marshall were elected aldermen.

Vonore Mayors, Past and Present
compiled by Brenda Tipton

Ward Barnes	1965-1969
Blanche Farnsworth	1969-1973
A.J. Kennedy	1973-1975
Blanche Farnsworth	1975-1977
Fred "Fizz" Tallent	1977-1983
Larry Summey	1983-1985
Fred "Fizz" Tallent	1985-1987
Larry Summey	1987-1989
Pearl Lashley	1989-1991
Marcus Kennedy	1991-1995
Fred "Fizz" Tallent	1995-2009
Larry Summey	2009-2014
Bob Lovingood	2014-Current

SOME POETRY

The following poem was written by Vonore community resident Gordon M. Cain, reportedly in 1965.

The Valley of the Little T

While I was visiting old Fort Loudon,
on the banks of the Little T,
I was overcome with the beauty,
of the valley surrounding me.
Strolling on through the secluded forest,
I stopped to admire a magnificent white oak tree.
While standing mystified with wonder,
it seemed the soft breeze said to me,
"Would you like to hear the story,
of the crafty Cherokee?
How abundant wildlife roamed the forest,
and the Indians worked the land?
Now this wonderful creation of nature,
faces destruction by greedy man.
O, children of the coming generation,
have pity on the likes of me.

We fought a bitter battle,
to save this priceless valley,
and the ancient homeland,
of the honorable Cherokee."
History will record this tragic story,
and the coming generation will see,
why we tried so hard to save this valley,
and our ancient history.
Now, if you would like to hear my story,
visit our Fort and see.
I am sure you will get the message,
from the mighty white oak tree.

Thanks for your interest in the people of Vonore. If you enjoyed the book, tell a friend and consider posting a brief review on the book's Amazon page.

For information on this or future editions, email lead editor Matt Deaton at Matt@MattDeaton.com.

And you are hereby cordially invited to visit the Vonore Heritage Museum (downtown by the new Veterans Memorial Park). There you'll find longtime Vonore barber Rue Frerichs's chair, Vonore Blue Devil sports memorabilia, Vonore Veteran uniforms, pictures and artifacts from various eras of Vonore's rich history. If you're a VHS alum, you might even find your picture on the wall.

Vonore Heritage Museum
611 Church St. Vonore, TN
call 423-884-2989 to confirm hours of operation

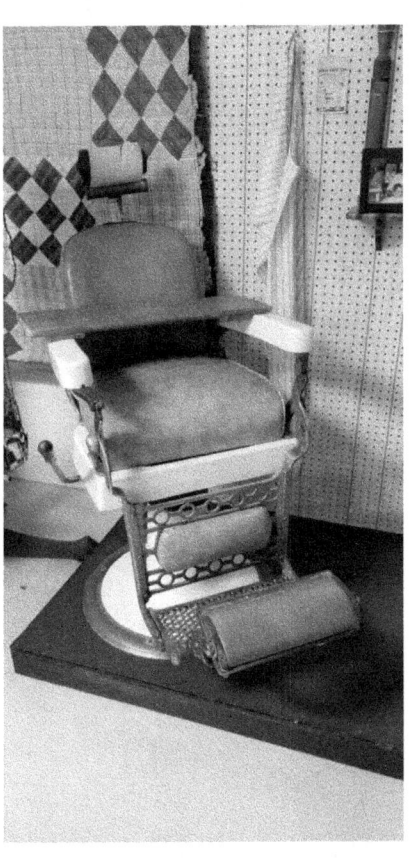

www.ingramcontent.com/pod-product-compliance
Lightning Source LLC
Chambersburg PA
CBHW071117160426
43196CB00013B/2598